Praise f

'Owen uses his ye to help us look at our lives and happiness in a clear and practical way. A brilliant book of intelligent advice and detailed case studies that encourages reflection and positive change.'
Fearne Cotton

'A refreshingly practical guide to finding joy every day.'
Susanna Reid

'Owen is an expert at showing, in his brilliantly down-to-earth way, how we can find happiness in the real world.'
Rob Rinder, aka Judge Rinder

'From mindfulness to interpersonal therapy you'll learn some of the most empowering solutions in how to move forward with your life.'
The Sun

'A fuss free and friendly hand in cultivating a positive and healthy headspace.'
***Magic Radio* Book Club**

ABOUT THE AUTHOR

Owen O'Kane has dual medical and psychotherapy training and is a former NHS Clinical Lead for Mental Health. His first book *Ten to Zen* was a *Sunday Times* bestseller. Owen lives in London but grew up in Belfast during The Troubles, which he describes as a great training ground for his current work. He also spent many years of his career working with people living with a terminal illness, which has greatly influenced his work. When not writing books, Owen runs his private therapy practice, delivers talks and contributes to press and media on mental wellness issues. He is a lover of dogs.

Also by Owen O'Kane:

Ten to Zen

TEN TIMES HAPPIER

OWEN O'KANE

ONE PLACE. MANY STORIES

HQ
An imprint of HarperCollins*Publishers* Ltd
1 London Bridge Street
London SE1 9GF

www.harpercollins.co.uk

HarperCollins*Publishers*
1st Floor, Watermarque Building, Ringsend Road,
Dublin 4, Ireland

This edition 2021

21 22 23 24 25 LSC 10 9 8 7 6 5 4 3 2 1
First published in Great Britain by
HQ, an imprint of HarperCollins*Publishers* Ltd 2020

Copyright © Owen O'Kane 2020

Owen O'Kane asserts the moral right to be
identified as the author of this work.
A catalogue record for this book is
available from the British Library.

ISBN: 9780008485009

Typeset in Bembo by Palimpsest Book Production Ltd, Falkirk, Stirlingshire

Printed and bound in the United States of America by
LSC Communications

All rights reserved. No part of this publication may be reproduced, stored in a retrieval system, or transmitted, in any form or by any means, electronic, mechanical, photocopying, recording or otherwise, without the prior permission of the publishers.

This book is sold subject to the condition that it shall not, by way of trade or otherwise, be lent, re-sold, hired out or otherwise circulated without the publisher's prior consent in any form of binding or cover other than that in which it is published and without a similar condition including this condition being imposed on the subsequent purchaser.

This is dedicated to the memory of my friend Nicholas who knew what mattered in life. He taught me to keep it simple.

CONTENTS

Introduction — 1

1. Stop Looking Back, You're Not Going That Way — 9
2. Get Out of Your Head — 37
3. No Regrets — 59
4. The Worry Trap — 87
5. Hell is Other People — 113
6. Kick the Habit — 143
7. Stop Blaming and Take Responsibility — 171
8. Comparison is the Thief of Joy — 199
9. High-Drama Living — 227
10. Living in the Now — 251
11. Resetting After Tough Times — 273

Epilogue: It Takes Work But It's Worth It — 299
Resources — 305
Acknowledgements — 317

INTRODUCTION

Do you ever feel disappointed with your life and have a sense that you could be happier than you currently are? If so, I believe that this is fully achievable on the condition that you are willing to let go of some of the stuff in life that's holding you back.

This belief, based on my twenty-five years' experience working in frontline physical and mental health services, motivated me to write *Ten Times Happier*. Whatever your story, I believe you can be happier than you are now, whether that's twice as happy or ten times happier!

Working as a therapist I see people suffering

every day. It's possible life may have dealt you some very harsh cards. But have you ever considered that you, unwittingly, might be adding to your suffering more than you realize? I truly believe this is one of the key reasons people struggle in life. You have a powerful role in turning this around.

I want to be honest from the start: if you are expecting a quick-fix, hoping-and-wishing, affirmation-based approach to finding happiness, you won't find it here. I'm not that type of person or therapist. What I *am* is passionate about helping people lead happier, more fulfilled lives by teaching them to understand why they struggle, and how they can move forward.

Reading this book in itself will not change your life but acting on the solutions will. I can promise you that.

ABOUT ME

If I'm offering solutions for a happier life, then I owe it to you to tell you some of my story.

I am a psychotherapist trained in several types of therapy that can help with managing 'everyday life' problems, emotions and the mind. I have a dual medical and psychotherapy background with over twenty-five years' experience of working in healthcare, some of which I spent caring for the terminally ill, and some working as a clinical lead for an NHS mental health service in London.

I am also a writer. My first book *Ten to Zen* tackled finding calm in life. I wanted this new book to look at happiness because, let's be honest, who doesn't want to be happier?

Outside of my professional life, I know what it's like to struggle. It's what drew me to my job. I think it's important to tell you this. I am not a person who lives in a constant bubble of smiling joy and platitudes. That would be painful to inflict on anyone.

I grew up in Belfast, Northern Ireland, during The Troubles, within an ordinary working-class family. It was a very traumatic time for me living in what can be best described as a war zone for most of my formative years.

I was also badly bullied in my youth, with a sense of not fitting in – which I later discovered was the result of my sexuality making me feel different – playing a huge part in my early story. Trust me when I say that being Irish, Catholic and gay back in the Seventies, Eighties and Nineties was not a walk in the park. I guess it was a 'triple threat' of sorts. That said, there was also a lot of love around which kept me sane.

I left Ireland in my early twenties for London, where I met my partner Mark, and we now live together with our dog, Kate. Over the years, I have developed my career, travelled the world and worked hard at turning a difficult past into a learning experience. I had to unlearn and let go of many things. I believe in making the best of my life. I also believe happiness is important.

In summary, happiness didn't come easy for me, so everything I'm talking about in this book, I say as a professional and as a person who has walked the walk!

HAPPINESS

When I talk about happiness, I don't want to offer a definition of what happiness will look like for you. I don't think anyone can do that. You will know what a happier life will look like, whether that's feeling more content, free, relaxed, unburdened, or authentic. It could be one thing; it may be many.

For me, I am happiest when I am at ease with

myself and the people in my life. It's not always a natural state. Sometimes it can go away, of course, but thankfully I know the way back. This is ultimately what I want to share with you. Getting you back on track to your happiness, whatever that means. But it involves effort, commitment and willingness to start letting go of the things that get in your way. I'll explain.

HOW DOES THIS BOOK WORK?

When I was planning this book, I agonized over how I would structure it in a way that was meaningful and would make sense to everyone who would read it. I had an epiphany moment one day when I was out walking my dog. To be honest, I was clearing up the dog's poop when a question came to mind: 'What do most people you treat struggle with?' And that laid the foundation for this book!

We are all driven by three systems at any given moment:

- **Threat**: anxiety, fear, protective mechanisms, guarded behaviours, avoidance

- **Drive**: achieving, distracting, fast living, substances to help us cope
- **Soothe**: self-soothing strategies that help us manage life (e.g. meditating, time out, self-compassion, soothing voice)

Almost every person I have ever treated in therapy wants to be a little happier. Most are driven by the threat and drive systems which are not in balance, and few of them can self-soothe. Despite coming to me with vastly different stories, almost 100 per cent of my clients have presented with similar themes that interfere with their happiness. Directly or indirectly they all link to the threat and drive systems being activated.

I've identified the top ten key themes:

1. The past
2. The mind
3. Regrets
4. Worry
5. Other people
6. Unhelpful behaviours
7. Blaming
8. Comparing
9. Addiction to drama
10. The future

All of these behaviours and preoccupations contribute significantly to feelings of unhappiness. I believe for each one you tackle – by engaging more with your soothing system along with more adaptive coping strategies, which I'll be teaching you – you have the opportunity to be happier than when you started.

Throughout the book you will work through a four-step process for dealing with each area by looking at:

- Why you are struggling and what the underlying psychological processes are
- Solutions for how to move forward
- What commitment is required
- How this will improve your life and contribute to your happiness.

The only requirements are an open mind and allowing a little time to think over the material I'm presenting. It will also be useful to have a notebook to use as a journal so you can write down your thoughts and record your progress at various points.

I wholeheartedly believe there will be insights here that will help shape your life and future happiness.

A FEW PRACTICALITIES

I have changed the names and amended details of any clients, stories or case studies mentioned in the book. This is to protect anonymity and of course respect the stories of people involved. Any similarities are purely coincidental.

Whilst I hope this book can offer great help and support to you, please always seek professional guidance and support if you are struggling to manage. The book isn't therapy in itself but offers tools to help you cope and move forward with the areas that are keeping you stuck. I provide a list of support organizations at the end of the book.

But for now, let's get started as we move to the first chapter on your journey to a happier life.

CHAPTER 1

STOP LOOKING BACK, YOU'RE NOT GOING THAT WAY

It was week four of a twelve-week group programme for ten very depressed clients. I was a newly qualified therapist in the early days of my career. I had a nice circle of chairs set up and a scented candle burning, and I was even wearing my therapist cardigan. What could go wrong? In short, everything! All of the clients in the group were angry, frustrated and disillusioned with everything, and that included me. I was stuck and they were stuck. The only comfort in the room was the wafting smell of the lavender and ginger candle.

Suddenly one of the participants, Angela, a recently divorced mum of two young children, declared, 'Therapy is bullsh★t, all we do is sit and complain.' There was rapturous applause from the group and there it was, my therapist light bulb moment.

I had an intuitive urge to ask everyone in the group to stand up, which I did. In truth I wasn't quite sure what I was going to do with them but I knew I had to do something. I had to think on my feet, knowing that the 'Hokey Cokey' or a group hug wasn't going to cut it in this instance. Trust me, ten angry, depressed clients are not an easy audience and I momentarily felt like I was in the lion's den!

Then something quite magical happened. As the group stood up they suddenly quietened and a new mood of curiosity entered the room. Doing what any therapist would do, I commented on the change of atmosphere. A reply soon followed from Angela: 'Well, at least now we're doing something to get us out of this mess.' It was the *doing something* that opened the door to new possibilities.

More quick thinking was required on my part. I realized the only props I had in the room were a window looking out onto a nice view of some trees and a dark, crumbling wall on the other side of the room. I decided these polar opposite views would be my tools. The window would represent a future that looked more hopeful and the dark wall would represent all the difficulties in the past that helped maintain depression.

I asked the entire group to form a line while I explained to them what the window and the wall represented. Then I asked them to turn towards the side of the room that represented what they would like therapy to focus on. Almost perfectly synchronized, they all turned towards the window. There was silence as they looked out onto the trees and a tangible sense of calm entered the room.

I then asked them where they felt their attention was focussed most of the time in everyday life. Again, perfectly synchronized, without hesitancy, they all turned towards the wall. None of the group said anything as they continued to stare at the wall. After a moment's silence, I asked a simple question: 'What do you think might be the problem with spending a lot of time focussed on the wall?'

This time the reply came from John, a twenty-four-year-old who rarely spoke in the group.

John's career as a professional sportsman had ended suddenly after an accident caused serious injuries. He felt hopeless and was struggling to move forward with his life. He gently said, 'If I stay stuck looking at this wall, I have my back turned to the future.'

And at that moment, amazingly, everyone independently and unprompted turned back towards the window, some slowly, some reluctantly, and some more deliberately. This was to be our focus in therapy for the remaining weeks.

We agreed together as a group that the dark wall would always be there but rather than ignore or deny it, they would learn from those dark past experiences to help them move forward.

Working with this group changed how I worked as a therapist. Early in my therapist's career I truly became aware of the detrimental impact of holding on to the past. What I noticed most was that my clients were either trapped going over events from their past or felt they had to follow unsustainable rules they'd created as a means of self-protection during or following unpleasant past events. When they started to let go of what no longer served a purpose, symptoms of depression lifted like a fog and happiness emerged from a place of great darkness. The entire group began to recover as, step by step, they started to let the past be.

It was incredibly humbling and a privilege to be part of this process of healing. Each week the atmosphere in the room lightened, laughter increased and at the final session everyone in the group brought an item that would remind them of the process. I was struck most by one woman, Jean, who brought a blank white page. She held it up and said, 'I've brought this today because I have a chance to write a new, more hopeful story.'

There was a sudden cheer from the group, a few tears and a tangible sense of optimism in the room. A completely different atmosphere from twelve weeks earlier. I should mention that I ditched the cardigan and scented candle.

There's a good reason that the first chapter of this book focuses on the past. Everyone reading this will have 'stuff' from the past that is getting in the way of life today. It could be violence in the family, bullying as a child, poverty, hardship, abuse, rejection, disappointments, failures, or things that didn't work out. The list is endless, as is the impact! It's not only the events that create issues though; it is also the rules and beliefs we learn from our past that sometimes keep us stuck. For some this can be like living in a straitjacket, with little psychological flexibility. I'll talk more about this later.

By the same token, almost every client I work with arrives at therapy feeling trapped in the past. Often, they have no idea how to get free. Many years back, I myself arrived in therapy for the first time, aged twenty-two. I thought I needed some help with worry and told the therapist I was otherwise 'pretty sorted'. Boy, was I in for a surprise! I started to explore how my past was impacting on me and realized why I was almost paralyzed with fear. Therapy was the most liberating experience of my life. Ironically my therapist was a nun and a truly amazing woman. I worried at the time she might be judgemental or be the wrong fit for me. That fear subsided when she said, 'You've had a pretty sh*t time, and deserve more. Let's put away the stuff you don't need. I think it's time for you to shine.' I have never forgotten that.

Back to the past: I'm not advocating that you attempt to simply erase from your mind any difficult stuff from your past and pretend it hasn't happened. That doesn't help. Indeed, my experience is that it can make things worse. Yet I believe you can begin to come to terms with your past and learn to manage it. You can become victorious rather than victimized. You can flourish rather than flounder. All of this is a choice. Your past can be a teacher, a motivator, an influencer, and part of your successes. But you need to allow it to do that.

It's important for me to be honest with you from

the outset. There are no magic wand solutions to moving forward from your past. It's not a case of repeating a mantra and your issues are all gone. I wish it were that simple. I believe that unless you deal with your past, your future happiness is compromised. With that in mind, I have developed a four-step approach that will help you navigate your way through this.

Using this process, I will be teaching you how to let go of what's holding you back. The four steps are:

1. Understanding why you become stuck
2. How you can move forward
3. How this will contribute to a happier life
4. Commitment to making the necessary changes.

Let's be honest, you won't want to read another sentence of this book unless there is something for you to take away. I promise there is much for you to take away that will change how you live your life. This book does not just provide understanding. It will provide guidance and insight on *how* to detach from the stuff that is getting in the way of your life and your happiness. The past is a good place to start.

WHY YOU BECOME STUCK

I want to start with some questions, and the reason for this is that they may link closely with your past. It's important to understand that. Take a little time to ponder these statements and ask yourself if any of them resonate with you:

- I often have thoughts that are self-critical, self-judgemental or self-deprecating. I'm hard on myself
- I avoid taking risks
- I worry a lot
- I find it hard to like myself
- I soothe my emotions with drink, drugs, shopping, gambling or sex
- I ruminate on the past a lot
- I feel flat and lack motivation
- I feel stuck
- I avoid people, places or new situations
- I get angry quickly
- I worry I'm repeating negative patterns I've witnessed
- I compare my life to those of others
- I seek validation and reassurance from others

- I feel dissatisfied with my life
- I get overwhelmed sometimes.

If one or all of these statements ring a bell with you, then welcome to your humanity. All of the above are likely closely linked with experiences or learnings from your past so this chapter will have something to say to you.

Most people are struggling with something, but they tend not to share it on Facebook, Instagram or Snapchat. I encourage you when reading this book to be mindful that you are in good company, with many readers (and the writer) tuned in to your struggle. As the old saying goes, 'We are all in the same boat.' I'm simply offering some oars, life jackets, and a few flares to get you on your way.

The problem with the past is that it lays the foundations for some challenging behaviours or unhelpful patterns that you might have developed in your current life. Most of the negative thoughts and emotions we experience – anxiety, depression, anger, addiction or hopelessness – can be linked to past experiences. The past is often what keeps current negative patterns alive. The two areas of the past that I witness people struggle with most are:

1. Unhelpful rules or beliefs that they have learnt or inherited
2. Negative or traumatic experiences.

I will tackle these separately as they both require individual attention.

RULES AND BELIEFS

Rules about how you live your life *can* be helpful but, unfortunately, many are not, especially if they are inflexible or create distress in your life. I'll share a personal example. In my own life as an Irish Catholic I was taught to always be a good person (with the threat of going to hell if I wasn't). That was the rule I was taught to abide by. The upside of this is I try to lead a decent life. The flipside is that I learnt how to be hard on myself. Sometimes I experience unnecessary guilt and so I have had to work towards unlearning this rule. I sometimes joke when I'm giving a talk that my personal mantra used to be, 'If it feels good, it must be bad.'

As children, we are not in a position to know what we can let go of. We simply inherit all of these rules and beliefs from families, cultures or religions. But that doesn't make them right or healthy.

I suggest that you stop to reflect on some of the rules or beliefs that impact negatively on your life. Remember, not all rules are bad. Some can be beneficial. Focus here on the rules in your life that feel restrictive for you. They usually tend to be prefaced by *should* or *must*. I'll explore later in the chapter how to *let go* of these influences from your past.

Examples of some unhelpful rules I hear every day in therapy are:

- I must be perfect
- I must not fail
- I must never disappoint
- I should be better
- I must never do anything wrong
- I must be the best
- I should succeed at everything
- I must be a good person.

It is also important to be aware that these beliefs can also flow into how you believe other people should be or behave. For example, if you have a belief you should be perfect, then you might have unrealistic expectations of everyone else. This is never much fun for the partners of perfectionists!

Take a moment here to write down in your

journal a few of the rules or beliefs that create challenges for you and make life a struggle at times. The easiest way to do this is to look firstly at the areas you struggle with in life. You can then figure out how your rules might be influencing that. This will then enable you to make decisions about which of those rules serve a positive purpose in your life and which don't. Take your time with this and don't be surprised if you feel emotional at times. This is totally normal.

NEGATIVE OR TRAUMATIC EXPERIENCES

These experiences are past events you had no control over, which led to damage and hurt in your present life. Only *you* will know what these events are. As a general rule they tend to feature regularly in your thoughts, impact on your happiness, deplete your self-worth and leave you with a prevailing sense of powerlessness. The most common events from the past I hear people discuss are:

- Abuse of all kinds (emotional, physical, sexual)
- Violence
- Poverty

- Deprivation
- Family conflict
- Addictions
- Bullying
- Cultural conflict
- Hardship.

The list is endless and again I would encourage you for now to simply make a note of any negative or traumatic experiences you would like to start letting go of. In summary, if the event still replays regularly in your mind, creates distress, and impacts on your happiness then you haven't let it go. In therapy we would say the event hasn't been processed.

HOW YOU CAN MOVE FORWARD

UNHELPFUL RULES AND BELIEFS

Earlier in the chapter you will have listed some of your unhelpful rules or beliefs learnt from past experiences. I want to keep this really simple by asking you to go back to your rules and for each of them ask:

1. Do these rules work for me?
2. Are they achievable all the time?

If not, then it's time to re-evaluate and make them more flexible. Remember, as I mentioned earlier, not all rules or beliefs are unhelpful but if they lack flexibility, therein lies the problem.

I worked with a client recently who had very strong rules and beliefs about being a 'good person'. He did laugh in a therapy session one day when I highlighted that Mother Teresa would have struggled to live with some of his rules! He worked as a fulltime carer, volunteered in a soup kitchen five days a week and sang in the church choir.

His belief was that he should always help people and put others first. If he didn't, he then saw himself as a bad person. It won't surprise you that he arrived in therapy exhausted, frustrated and unfulfilled. He was operating from a belief that to be a good person he had to do good all the time. It wasn't sustainable. Ultimately, he had to learn that he was a good enough person whether or not he engaged in all these activities.

As you look at your rules from earlier I would encourage you now to consider introducing some flexibility to some of the more rigid rules you might have. For example, the rule, *I must be perfect*, could now become, *I don't need to be perfect all the time*. Likewise, *I must never disappoint people*, could now become, *sometimes it's OK to say no*. If it's helpful for you, write your new flexible rules down in your journal so you can remind yourself of them when needed.

Be mindful that this work takes time and patience. You are rewiring your brain to respond more flexibly. Sometimes you will fail and want to return to the safety of what you are familiar with but stay focussed on the new freedom and flexibility this will eventually bring.

You are now giving yourself the opportunity to rewrite the rules from your past, and make the new rules work for you. You are no longer living by the unhelpful inherited rules that simply don't work for you.

It is important to be mindful that you can respect the inherited rules of your past but you don't have to agree with them.

Living your life by rules that are not comfortable for you is tough. It's almost like walking through life in a pair of shoes that are the wrong size. It will be uncomfortable, restrictive and painful at times. You now have the option of choosing a more comfortable fit. Take it from me, I've spent many years wearing size seven hobnail boots, when a pair of size nine loafers would have been a much better fit.

NEGATIVE OR TRAUMATIC EXPERIENCES

Some negative or traumatic past experiences will get in the way of your life if they are not dealt with. I am confident some of what I offer you here will be immensely helpful and allow you to move forward. It is worth mentioning some long-standing deep issues from the past may need discussion with a professional, simply to help you process the events and leave them in the past. Not everyone needs therapy, but some people do. There is no right or wrong here. Simply be aware that there are options for how you decide to manage this section of our work together. If self-help work isn't enough, always seek professional guidance.

The approach I use to help process a difficult experience or event from the past encourages you to ask yourself five key questions about that event in the here and now:

1. **Ruminating.** Is there any benefit to holding on to this hurt from the past?

2. **Self-judgement.** Was it your fault this painful event or circumstance took place?
3. **Expectations of self.** At the time of the event can you accept it would have been difficult to have the perfect mindset to deal with it?
4. **Self-blaming.** Did you wish for this event or experience, which ultimately had a negative impact, to happen?
5. **Mindful awareness.** Can you accept the actual event is in the past and you are now safe?

In the vast majority of cases the answer to all or some of these questions is likely to be no. But no matter how many you answer no to, the main aim is learning to stop with any self-judgement or self-blame, which can often accompany these experiences.

What I know from the hundreds of clients I have treated over the years is that holding on to the past causes one thing only: pain. My interest is in easing that pain and I believe the solution lies in the five alternative options below which link to the questions I have just asked. For example, if harsh self-judgement is one of your patterns, then you have the option to drop this and replace it with something more helpful. Below are some of the alternatives I propose you take on board. You will know what resonates with you.

I suggest you reflect on a past event that troubles you and work through each of the five points below with the event in mind. It will help you find a new perspective.

FIVE ALTERNATIVE OPTIONS FOR MANAGING THE PAST

1. You don't need to replay this event over and over again. That achieves nothing other than keeping you stuck in the past. If you are unable to stop replaying it, this is when professional support is important.
2. Ease up with the self-judgement. Self-blaming or punishment is never helpful.
3. Remember whatever happened, it's over now and you have survived.
4. Taking care of yourself is of utmost importance. Do this with compassion.
5. None of what has happened can be changed now. You deserve a happier future.

HOW THIS WILL CONTRIBUTE TO A HAPPIER LIFE

Learning to manage the past will liberate you and allow you to experience a new sense of empowerment. When I talk about 'managing the past', I am encouraging you to use these techniques that will help you file away memories that are no longer needed in the here and now. You will no longer be controlled by unhelpful or painful aspects of your past. Instead the past can now become a teacher, a tool for wisdom.

THE EVIDENCE AND RESEARCH

What we know from all the major research papers on depression and other mood 'disorders' is that one of the strongest factors for maintaining low mood is ruminating on the past. Let me explain this a little more. In short, if you replay the same material in your mind over and over again, then you are reliving the experience in an unhelpful way. If you are feeling low or want to avoid negative changes in your mood then scientifically the evidence is clear: don't overthink the past. Overthinking will not change what has happened, it will not lead to a resolution, and it will keep you stuck. If you still feel stuck after following the steps in this chapter or it seems impossible to not think about events, that is when professional help might be considered to help you process whatever is going on.

It's a similar story with anxiety. Many of the latest neuroscientific developments on mindfulness indicate that living in the present moment deactivates the brain's threat centre (the amygdala) and reduces symptoms of anxiety. When excessive time is spent focussing on the past then the present moment gets lost, leading to rising anxiety levels.

Almost all of the research into self-esteem has also clearly shown that when people do not challenge or restructure unhelpful rules or beliefs from the past then self-esteem issues become more prominent in adult life.

In short, if you dwell too much on traumatic events of the past or unhelpful rules and beliefs, you can be robbed of your future. I present to you a choice: a future nourished by your past or one that is sabotaged by it.

COMMITMENT

I hold a belief that changes don't happen in life unless we commit to them. Imagine you were to move forward focussed on building a hopeful future, with the same energy that you've previously dedicated to your past. Can you visualize how much power you would reclaim? Can you see how much potential there is? You have the chance to rewrite the script of your life. Can you see what an amazing opportunity that is?

With that in mind I invite you now to write down in your journal your commitment to yourself. What will you do to help you engage less with the unhelpful parts of your past?

For example, you could consider how you reduce time spent thinking over events. What items that activate unhelpful memories could you dispose of? How can your behaviour towards yourself change? What have you learnt from the events? How will you treat yourself more compassionately going forward? What rules can you drop, amend or tweak?

CASE STUDY

In the introduction, I promised some real-life case stories on how my approach impacts and influences lives for the better. In my line of work as a psychotherapist I have learnt that you sometimes must be brave enough to appropriately share parts of your own story and that's what I want to start by doing. It is often easy for professionals like me to hide behind our titles. However, we are human beings. We are all in this life together, making our way through and trying to make sense of it all. If I am going to invite you to listen to my teachings and experiences, then I equally owe it to you to share some of my story at times.

When I was a young boy I was severely bullied at school. I was different from the other kids in Belfast. I was learning to play piano, loved the theatre and never quite understood why the other boys wanted to run after a ball as a means of entertainment! I'm still working on that. Of course, they didn't understand me either. I was the 1970s equivalent of Billy Elliot minus the dance moves. I lived in a world of make-believe, while many of the other kids were living in a different world.

After many years of bullying, rejection and humiliation, I started to ask questions such as, 'Am I good enough? Am I the problem? Why don't I fit it?' I wasn't happy.

Fast-forward to my adult years and of course this part of my past travels with me, like a hanger-on at a party. I realize that I sometimes doubt myself and feel anxious. It was in my own therapy I discovered that I didn't have to live by some of my inherited rules and beliefs about fitting in or pleasing people. I discovered I was good enough and that the problem wasn't me. Other people who couldn't tolerate difference were the problem.

If I had made the choice to continue listening to this message from my past then I wouldn't have gone to university, created a nice life and become a successful therapist and writer. I made the conscious decision to acknowledge the hurt this part of my past caused but it didn't have to define my future or block my happiness. I had to practise the letting go I talk about. I had to learn new flexible rules and most importantly I had to learn to accept and like myself. Happiness for me truly is an 'inside job'.

Another part of my past also worth sharing is my growing up in Northern Ireland during The Troubles. Living in Belfast during an intense period of bombs and bullets was a scary experience. I learnt from a very young age that life wasn't safe and threat was everywhere. To be fair, during that time there was some truth in this. Yet when I moved away from Northern Ireland I had to learn to start letting go of this part of my past otherwise all of life would appear a threat. It's difficult to feel happy if under threat.

When I moved to London I went to see my first ever West End show with a friend. I was ecstatic and the moment of entering the theatre was one of the best of my life. This was the stuff I had dreamt of as a child. However, it was short lived. The opening scene of the play had an unexpected gunshot sound and I instantly jumped to the floor. No one else budged! Yes, all my street credibility was lost in a moment and you can imagine some of the strange glances from the surrounding audience as they wondered about the strange man on the floor.

That strange man on the floor was hardwired to fear loud bangs, traumatized from an early life of bombs in Belfast. I had to relearn that not all loud noises were a threat. My anxious brain had to be rewired from earlier traumas. This was a part of my past I had to deal with.

Experience has taught me to use this part of my past in my work as a therapist to help other people manage anxiety. I didn't have to be defined by a negative aspect of my past. Neither do you. Whatever has happened in your past, it doesn't have to define you.

There is a wise expression: 'Don't look back, you're not going that way.' Sometimes we have to look back but it doesn't mean we should keep looking there. The people in my depression therapy group decided to stop looking back and it became their way forward. I now pass this insight on to you. The past is over. You can rewrite your rules. You can let go of the difficult stuff. You are not going that way any more.

Where we will go next, though, is to your mind. Together we can explore how it may also be getting in the way of your happiness and what you can do about that.

SUMMARY

- Negative past experiences that have not been dealt with can get in the way of your happiness.
- Some of the rules and beliefs inherited from your past may not serve you well now.
- Learning to let go of difficult past events will bring you a new sense of freedom.
- Learning to create new, flexible rules and beliefs will offer psychological flexibility. This will contribute to your happiness.
- You have a choice to take control and not be dominated by the darker parts of your past.

CHAPTER 2

GET OUT OF YOUR HEAD

Have you ever stopped to consider that your mind, and how you relate to it, might play an enormous role in how happy you are? With absolute confidence, I can assure you it does. My mind once sabotaged my happiness on a mindfulness retreat! I'll explain.

I had always thought of myself as a mindful and pretty chilled kind of guy. That was until I attended a mindfulness teacher-training course.

It was an intensive retreat over nine days, with very early starts and late finishes – often after 10 p.m. Most meals were in silence and large parts of the day were spent practising mindfulness. Set in a beautiful location in the heart of the countryside, it should have been the perfect place for calm. We were privileged to have the inspirational Melanie Fennell (a very respected figure in the world of therapy and mindfulness) as our coach – and her words 'just notice' played a huge part in my training. But calm didn't come easy.

Before the course I had envisaged nine days of peace and tranquillity leading to a blissful state of contentment. But I was wrong. Once I had the space to breathe and find silence, I discovered that my mind didn't stop.

- If it wasn't worrying, then it was planning.
- If it wasn't thinking about the future, then it was replaying the past.
- If it had nothing to do, then it would start wondering what was for dinner or what the other participants were doing.

I thought I was a pretty calm person, but I was astounded to discover I had a mind on overdrive that didn't quite know how to slow down.

The experience was uncomfortable but an incredible breakthrough. My mind was getting in the way of *living* and of my *happiness*. And this realization was swiftly followed by another – that

I would now be a lot better at being able to identify with, and help, my clients for whom this was also a problem.

The volume of the noise in my head was astounding. For example, it was day four of the course and I was seated ready for a forty-five-minute guided mindful meditation. The focus was compassion. I had been looking forward to this meditation and had made a decision that it was going to be a perfect, peaceful one.

This was not the case. Even before the meditation started, I was irritated with my position in the room, as it was close to a door. I had planned to arrive on time to get a better seat but I'd been delayed. This started a self-attack in my head: 'You idiot, why did you arrive so late?' There wasn't much compassion happening at this stage!

And it got worse. My next irritation was a person close to me breathing too loudly, followed by a cramp in my leg, and then my tummy started to gurgle louder than it has ever done in my life. The noise in my head got louder, the self-criticism strengthened and suddenly I was telling myself this was all a waste of time. I was deflated, disappointed and by that stage I just wanted to give up on the course. Here I was, a therapist on meditation training, and I couldn't get the basics right.

When the meditation session had ended, I had an opportunity to discuss the experience with my mentor. I described what happened and to my surprise, she smiled. 'Wow,' she said. 'Sounds like a great meditation.'

I was stunned. What was so great about that? But as she explained, it *was* a great meditation because I had noticed my mind. I had noticed all of the activity and frustration. But it hadn't stopped me trying to meditate. It was fine if I noticed all of the activity in my mind – noticing it didn't mean I had to engage with it. This was one of the most liberating moments of my life. I realized I needed to learn the skill of managing my mind and regulating the volume.

Our minds are at the centre of all our experiences. You are learning the skill of taking back control of your mind, so it doesn't take control of you.

WHY YOU BECOME STUCK

I believe that most human distress relates to what goes on in our minds. Regardless of the event, how we feel about it always links back to how our minds interpret it. That will always vary from person to person. Going on a roller coaster terrifies me, whereas my partner behaves like an excited child! Essentially, it's difficult to live a happy life if you haven't got a handle on your mind.

A client, Nick, who was struggling with anger issues and depression, described in a session with me an event in his life that perfectly illustrated this. One day, he was driving to work and he encountered a delay at a railway level crossing. Nick was only one car away from getting past the gate but just as he approached, the gate came down and he was forced to stop. Even though it is standard procedure for a gate to block traffic crossing the rail tracks when a train is passing through – in fact, it's vital for safety – he was furious. He got out and started to scream at the car in front of him for not driving fast enough. He kicked the gate at the level crossing and then returned to his car to persistently sound his horn until the train had passed and the gate was raised.

When we explored his actions, Nick was able to reflect that, at the time, his mind felt 'as if it were going to explode'. He wanted to get to his destination quickly and his mind was telling him:

- This is just your *bad luck*
- This shouldn't be happening

- You will be late getting to work
- Why do trains get priority?
- The driver in front of you caused the problem
- This isn't fair.

Nick had listened to these thoughts, started to engage with them and then responded by screaming, jumping out of his car, and sounding his horn continuously.

In this moment Nick's mind was inappropriately in threat mode. His amygdala, the centre in the brain that protects us from danger, was telling him there was a threat and he should react accordingly. There wasn't any real danger but his threat system reacted because something hadn't gone to plan. But by following the steps outlined on pages 47–9, Nick could have had a very different reaction. If Nick had allowed himself time and space to acknowledge but not to engage with the content of his mind, his thoughts would have been quieter and more flexible, and would perhaps have played out something like this:

- That's a shame but it's OK, I can wait
- Better to be safe than have an accident
- I'll listen to the radio while waiting.

The more Nick is able to practise this approach, then the easier it becomes for him longer term.

Can you see the difference in his thoughts? And how they in turn would have produced a very different reaction, too? If we believe everything our minds tell us it won't always produce a rational, sensible outcome.

UNDERSTANDING OUR MINDS A LITTLE MORE

We have around 60–80,000 thoughts per day according to neuroscientific research. Some of the research indicates that as much as 60 to 70 per cent of thought content can be negative in nature. When I say negative, let me give some context. Back in Neanderthal times it was helpful to have fearful protective thoughts as a means of staying safe from predatory animals. The problem is we have evolved as a species and we don't need as many of these types of thoughts to protect us any more.

It's important to understand that most of our thoughts are automated processes and link closely with our life experiences, culture, rules, beliefs and predisposition. This is how our neurological pathways develop thought patterns. In simple terms, we have often formed habitual ways of thinking that are the 'norm' for us but not necessarily helpful. Don't fret though because, like all habits, thought habits can be unlearnt.

Look at the statements below. They represent some habitual unhelpful thinking styles. How many of these are familiar to you? Take a little time with this to try to see how many you can personally identify with.

- I won't be able to do it
- I'm not good enough
- Nothing good ever happens to me
- Everything is terrible
- It has to be this way or I won't do it
- I think someone else will be better for the job
- This is a disaster
- It's not my problem
- This is not fair

It doesn't matter whether you tick one or all of the above, the important thing here is that you recognize your unhelpful thinking patterns. Let us explore a little further how these ways of thinking impact the mind.

- If you engage and cooperate with a mind that tells you you won't be able to do something, then in life you are unlikely to take any risks.
- If you listen to a mind that tells you that you're not good enough, then you will transmit that vibe to the world and those around you.
- If you take seriously a mind that tells you that nothing good happens for you, then you lose sight of any positive or joyful events that do occur.
- If you cooperate with a mind telling you everything is terrible, then life will feel terrible a lot of the time.
- If you abide with a mind instructing you that it has to be this way or nothing, then you become inflexible and rigid. This is an uncomfortable way to live.

Most of these negative ways of thinking are simply habits of thought, not facts. I am going to repeat that. *Most of what you think is thought, not fact.* The challenge is how you decide to relate to your thoughts. If you believe the content of your mind to be the gospel truth, then you will struggle, and happiness will be absent. The freedom comes when you decide not to believe absolutely everything your mind is telling you and when you realize what you can let go of.

Every person reading this book will have an area of their life that their mind is getting in the way of. It might be a relationship issue, making a change, going for a promotion, making a fresh start or taking a risk. I would encourage you to list now three key areas in your life that feel blocked or limited by your mind, your way of thinking.

Would you like your thoughts to have less hold over your life?

If yes, then you are halfway there. The motivation to change is a large part of the journey.

HOW YOU CAN MOVE FORWARD

Considering the complexity of the human mind, changing your thought patterns might seem like a mammoth task. But you can do it, using a few simple techniques.

I have developed a four-step method to change your thought patterns, which I will guide you through. To start with, this will feel unusual, as the brain will likely want to revert to old patterns. The trick is to persevere. You are teaching the mind to respond in a different way. In time, healthier responses will become the new normal.

STEP 1: ACKNOWLEDGE AN UNHEALTHY THOUGHT

Acknowledging an unhealthy thought pattern is a little like appeasing someone who wants to get your attention in some way. If you ignore them or push them away, they may keep coming back until their needs are met. When you acknowledge your mind, even while it is not operating in a functional or helpful way, you are immediately taking control of your thought patterns. You are saying to your mind, 'OK, I see you are there and I'm acknowledging you.' Automatically you take back a little control and break old patterns.

STEP 2: CREATE SPACE

When the mind is creating negative or unhelpful content you have a choice in how engaged you become with it. Remember, they are thoughts, not facts. During my time as a psychotherapist I have come across numerous techniques for creating space in the mind. My favourite is the 'movie director'.

Visualize your thoughts as if they are playing out on a movie screen. You are simply watching all of the content of your mind. You have two options:

1. Either you can climb into the movie set and engage with the action. It will produce lots of drama. It's not likely to prove helpful.
2. Or you can observe and watch the movie, like a director. Then decide on the content you want to let go of.

The second option will allow you space to stop and breathe rather than accepting your thoughts as true. Remember you are not overthinking or analyzing the thoughts, you are simply letting go. You are directing your mind. It is not directing you.

STEP 3: EXAMINE THE EVIDENCE

Sometimes the mind can create some harsh material for us to digest:

- You are rubbish
- You are a failure
- You are ugly
- You are stupid.

If you're going to listen to and engage with such content surely you owe it to yourself to ask whether it's 100 per cent true? And if so, where is the evidence?

When you think about it rationally, your mind likely won't be able to provide irrefutable evidence. And you have the opportunity to provide it with alternative evidence. Even if there are examples where things haven't gone to plan, this won't have happened every time. For example, the thought 'You are rubbish' can be challenged. You can provide examples from your life when you have succeeded, achieved, connected and loved. As there is plenty of evidence to suggest that you aren't rubbish, assuming 'I am rubbish' can't be an automatic process any more.

STEP 4: LET GO

The mind's unhelpful content often arrives with intensity and force. It can sometimes seem impossible to challenge it. However, this four-step process provides you with a strategic, disciplined approach to letting go of your unhelpful thoughts. Acknowledging the mind, creating space and examining the evidence places you in a perfect position to let go of the unhelpful thoughts. With practice and patience this process will become more routine.

The following tips may also be helpful to support this process.

- Try to lower the stress barometer of your life. The mind produces more intense thoughts when your emotional barometer is high and these are harder to step back from.
- High cortisol and adrenaline will speed up the mind and create more activity. Physical activities can help you burn off stress.
- Lifestyle or work–life balance is essential.
- Healthy foods reduce some excitability in the mind. Explore some of the online resources that have countless suggestions for healthy mind foods.

HOW THIS WILL CONTRIBUTE TO YOUR HAPPINESS

Research, particularly from the world of mindfulness and anxiety treatments, shows the benefits of this process. Disengaging from the unhelpful content of the mind leads to:

- Improved motivation
- Clearer thinking
- Improved decision making
- Better relationships
- Improved self-confidence
- Greater productivity
- Balanced moods
- A more rational perspective
- A calmer mind
- Clarity.

I am sure you would agree that in a world crowded with noise, creating space between you and your mind is a no-brainer (pardon the pun!). Who wouldn't want these benefits to lighten the load in a world full of challenges? We all spend way too much time attending to our minds' thoughts, believing that's where the answers are to be found. The reality is that the solution is often found in challenging those thoughts.

COMMITMENT

Remember, I am not saying you should never try to attend to your thoughts again! But if you're struggling, you are likely giving way too much attention to your negative thoughts. Committing to engaging less with these thoughts is an important act of self-care. Essentially, you are standing up to your mind's unhelpful thinking and saying, 'Enough is enough.' With this commitment, you will find empowerment and strength.

You will generally feel happier.

I invite you now to write down your commitment to yourself for what you will do to challenge negative thoughts. Remember, you are paying less attention to your mind because much of the negative content it creates is getting in the way of your life.

For example, the commitment could be: I commit to reminding myself that I am not the content of my mind and that thoughts are not facts.

Whether it's work, relationships, family matters, your future, how you look, your weight or any area that is causing you difficulty, the same rules apply for all. Engage less with the unhelpful thoughts.

CASE STUDY

Julie is a forty-year-old mum of two young children and working full-time as a bank manager. When she came to my private practice for therapy she was exhausted, anxious and not sleeping well. Her initial goal in therapy was to learn techniques to cope better at work as she was about to be promoted and take on more responsibility.

As I began working with Julie, I soon discovered that she was clearly a very competent, loving mum. She loved her husband and enjoyed her job. Her external world was relatively stable. Initially I wondered whether it was the sheer volume of responsibility that was causing her issues. We discussed boundaries, time management and all sorts of techniques. This wasn't helpful. Every week she would return to therapy in the same tired, anxious emotional state. We were clearly not on the right track.

It was around the fourth session when Julie came in, sat down and cried for nearly fifteen minutes before she spoke. When she had composed herself I asked her how she was. She replied, 'It's still the same.' I asked her what 'it' was. 'My mind.' I asked her to describe what that was like – and her description provided the solution.

Julie described a mind that was on hyper-alert the entire time: thinking, worrying, planning, wondering, questioning, doubting and self-criticising. Although her presentation was theoretically in line with diagnostic criteria for an anxiety disorder, I was less interested in labelling her with a diagnosis. For me, measurable improvement is much more important. It was very clear to me that the root of her current problem was linked to how she was relating to her mind. We explored this further. She was paying attention to *all* of her mind's activity. She was over-engaging with the thoughts, trying to work them out.

Despite the content of her mind – often self-critical thoughts – she eloquently described the tone of her mind. It was like a head mistress telling her she wasn't good enough and that she was failing at everything all of the time. Such thoughts were creating anxiety and exhaustion as she tried to battle them.

I asked Julie the following questions:

- Have you ever acknowledged your thoughts just as thoughts, not facts?
- Have you ever created any space between you and your thoughts?
- Have you ever examined the evidence as to whether these thoughts are true?
- Have you ever considered that you can let these thoughts go?

It will come as no surprise that the answer to every question was no. From that moment our agenda for therapy was set and Julie embarked on her journey to pay less attention to her negative thoughts. She worked on the techniques, practised between sessions and within a few weeks she started to improve considerably. Her anxiety dropped, her sleep improved and her energy returned. Julie was no longer a slave to her mind.

Julie's distress ultimately wasn't caused by the challenges of her external world but by her relationship with the internal wrangling of her mind.

Julie's story is not uncommon. Sometimes accepting negative thoughts as true without question is the primary problem but, more often than not, it is accompanied by other difficulties. Nevertheless, the mind is the epicentre of all our experiences, so mastering these techniques will liberate you in more ways than you can imagine.

If Julie's story strikes a chord with you, I encourage you to pay close attention to your commitment to the work in this chapter. While all of the work in each chapter is important, the mind's impact on our well-being can seem less obvious, but it is vital. Take control of your mind and you are on the road to regaining more joy in your life. Regrets will lessen, which, as it happens, is the next step on our journey: learning to manage regrets that are getting in the way of your life.

SUMMARY

- Thoughts are automated processes and many are negative in nature.
- Thoughts are not facts.
- Learning to stop, create space and observe the mind, rather than buying into its narrative, will ease distress.
- Always examine the evidence for negative or critical thinking.
- Happiness comes when you detach more from interacting with the mind's chatter and learn to become the peaceful observer.

CHAPTER 3

NO REGRETS

I bet you've 'got it wrong' at some points in your life. I think we all have at various stages. But isn't it an interesting phrase, seemingly so innocuous, yet the word 'wrong' has immediate connotations of blame. I think the word 'regret' has similar associations but with an added tone of disappointment.

When I worked in the world of palliative care I looked after an elderly woman, Mary, who lived alone with her two cats. She had just weeks to live and we developed a rapport in that short time. Mary was also Irish, and, like me, had made London her home. She'd never married, and described a very solitary, quiet life. She was determined to die at home and part of my role was to help support her in that wish. As I got to know her, I sensed Mary was burdened with something greater than her illness. She had accepted that she was dying and was resigned to it but something else was clearly troubling her.

One afternoon I paid her a visit and decided to share my concern. My instincts were correct. Mary tearfully began to share a story of regret, a story she had never told anyone else in her lifetime.

At the age of seventeen Mary discovered she was pregnant. She was an only child in her family and six months into the pregnancy she decided to inform her parents. As was common in Ireland at the time, Mary was forced by her parents to give the child up for adoption. A child out of wedlock was deemed shameful and her family wouldn't support her.

Mary's baby girl was taken from her at birth and two days later Mary set sail for London. She couldn't bear to stay in Ireland after the trauma of giving up her child. She never returned to Ireland. She described her agonizing lifelong secret and the regret of not standing up to her parents or escaping earlier without telling them of her pregnancy. This regret caused Mary an enormous amount of pain, loneliness and isolation. She never married because she believed she wasn't deserving of happiness.

Two weeks after telling me her story, Mary died. I cried driving home from work that day. Her story deeply touched me. Mary's regret dominated her life but it didn't have to be that way. If she had told someone years earlier about this regret, would her life have been different? I suspect an act of kindness or acceptance from someone or herself might have given her permission to stop punishing herself. She wasn't able to let go or come to terms with this regret. Consequently, she never allowed herself to truly experience happiness.

I think of life as a series of situations. Sometimes we misinterpret the information available or we lack clarity, leading to a decision or action we regret. As human beings we seem to have a real problem with allowing ourselves permission to make mistakes, and forgiving ourselves. This in turn impacts on our happiness.

Throughout the chapter, when I discuss regrets I do so without judgement, retribution, blame or shaming but instead in a spirit of openness, compassion, curiosity and learning. This is something I will also be encouraging you to do. Our regrets have the potential to shape us, just as they have the potential to break us. The freedom lies in knowing there is a choice in which direction you travel.

I have some regrets in my life. Opportunities missed, mistakes I've made, people I wish I'd treated better and conversations not had. The unhealthy Irish Catholic part of me will tell me that I've done wrong (if I allow it to). But the rational, emotionally intelligent part of me allows for a more flexible approach, enabling me to explore what I learnt from the regretful experiences in my life, and how they can influence my future.

As an aside, I should mention that any references I make to Irish Catholicism, a hugely influential part of my story, are not directly an attack on the Church or any religions. Some religions are doing some very important compassionate work to alleviate human suffering in the world. However, as a psychotherapist, I know that religions can also sometimes ignite shame with lots of fear-driven doctrine. This can be unhelpful for some and it was for me.

This chapter will explore why beating yourself up over regrets can impact detrimentally on your happiness and wellbeing. I will also teach you how to let go of the self-blaming aspect of regrets, adjust perspective, and show how this can contribute to a happier life.

Without doubt, every person who has stepped through the door of my therapy room has discussed regrets of some form or another. The exception is of course a patient with a very extreme narcissistic personality disorder or with some sort of delusional traits. Yet even then, when vulnerability is eventually accessed, some hurt will emerge linking to a regret. That said, in time some people reconcile with the regret naturally, while others don't. If you have got stuck in any way with regret, then it's important to know there is a way forward.

Here's the interesting thing. No matter what the regret is, if people hold on to it by overthinking it, and blaming and punishing themselves, they become stuck. Here are some of the common 'regrets' I have heard discussed most over the years. A top ten of sorts:

- Infidelity
- Losing temper
- Not being a good enough partner, son, daughter, parent, etc.
- Financial decisions and over-spending
- Keeping secrets
- Religious values not upheld
- Sexual activities
- Excessive alcohol, drugs, medication

- Wasted opportunities
- Treatment of another person

And here are the symptoms of holding on to regrets that I have witnessed:

- Excessive guilt
- Shame (thinking 'I am a bad, dirty, horrible person', etc.)
- Self-loathing
- Anger (often disproportionate to the event)
- Fear of risk
- Rumination (going over the mistake repeatedly, looking for new information)
- Repeating the same mistakes as part of a pattern
- Low self-worth
- Self-blaming
- Feeling defeated.

I would suggest you take a few moments out now to consider some of the regrets you have in your life. Make a note in your journal of the ones that bother you most, the regrets that lie in the pit of your core festering.

When you've done this, I suggest you also list the thoughts, feelings and behaviours that accompany these regrets. Some of these might mirror the symptoms listed above or you may have others. The key aim for now is simply to be aware that holding on to regret may be getting in the way of your happiness. There is an old adage: 'When you are aware, you are halfway there.' Awareness is a good thing to have.

At this point it's important to stress that I am not attempting to reframe every regret as a 'good thing'. Sometimes we say or do things that have the potential to hurt people and cause destruction. We have to take responsibility for that. But regret can be turned around and used positively to move you towards atonement or making amends. It can also provide the opportunity to see the good in a bad situation and grow as a person. The problem for some people is that regret can become a fixed emotional state. Understanding why this happens is our next step together.

WHY YOU BECOME STUCK

It is well documented that the human mind tends to automatically default to negative content, and this includes regrets.

Even if you interpret the regrets as a learning experience, the reality is that your conscience may decide that an action or words were 'wrong' or 'out of character' for you.

Your conscience, as well as evoking feelings of regret, can also help you gauge what is an appropriate emotional response in the wake of your behaviour and actions. For example, were you to shout at someone for accidentally parking across your driveway, then later in the day your conscience may make you regret your action. A healthy response to this may be feelings of appropriate guilt leading you to apologize or make amends to the injured party. This is what is known as an adaptive response or healthy regret. It is a five-part process:

- **Awareness.** What have I just done?
- **Reflection.** I shouldn't have done that.
- **Emotional response.** I'm feeling guilty.
- **Making amends.** I need to apologize or make amends.
- **Key learning.** How can I avoid this happening again and let this event go?

On the other hand, if we fast-forward to a few months later and you're still troubled by deep regret about the event, this is what an unhelpful maladaptive response, an unhealthy regret, would look like:

- **Awareness.** I still can't believe I did that.
- **Reflection.** I hate myself for doing that.
- **Emotional response.** I am ashamed. I'm a bad person.
- **Making amends.** Excessive attempts to prove worth.
- **Key learning.** No learning, instead shame, self-deprecation, self-punishment.

So it's clear there are differences in how you can manage the regrets in your life. In the example cited, a wrongdoing was carried out but the maladaptive response to that event would have a very different impact on your happiness and wellbeing long term compared to the adaptive response. In an ideal world, we would all automatically opt for the adaptive response. But the reality is a little more complex than that. I believe there are two reasons for this:

1. Most people have a number of regrets they carry around with them that lead to significant emotional burden. It's hard to think rationally when you are stressed by these emotional burdens.

2. We are programmed by various aspects of our existence (which I'll go into in more detail in the following paragraphs) as to how we respond to life events. Sometimes our automated programming is the unhelpful maladaptive type.

It's difficult to understand why we hold on to regrets, knowing that it achieves nothing but further misery. My belief, based on clinical experience, is that all our early experiences – family, school, attachments, religion, culture, and of course our genetic personality predisposition – contribute to how we respond. Some of the information that you have been programmed with will have been helpful and some not.

The way forward with this is identifying the unhelpful stuff so you can decide to detach from it and have more control over your response to regrets. Here are some learnt patterns you may have been programmed with that could be stopping you from moving past regrets. Take a moment here to work out if you identify with any of the patterns and make a note in your journal:

- **Perfectionism.** Everything, including you, has to be perfect.
- **Shame.** If you do wrong, you are bad, worthless.
- **Excessive criticism.** If you have done wrong, you deserve these feelings.
- **Self-punishment.** Mistakes should be self-punished.
- **Self-persecution.** Atonement for your mistake.
- **Inflexible thinking.** Black and white thinking style.
- **Self-worth.** You are the problem.
- **Blaming.** It's all your fault.
- **Not good enough.** This is just more proof you are not enough.

If you think back to your work on the past in Chapter 1, you'll notice links with these patterns. All of the work within each chapter will interlink at some point. As humans, we are a little like jigsaws, piecing together the different parts of our story.

It may also be helpful to list your top three regrets, the ones that you can't let go of, and reflect on which of the above patterns have prevented you from letting go in a healthy way. I suggest you explore with curiosity *how* the patterns above may contribute to you getting stuck in regret, and consider whether there may be room for more flexibility with these particular patterns.

Before you do this, here is an example from a client of mine that may be helpful for you. Ruth, a twenty-five-year-old woman I was treating in therapy, struggled with guilt and shame linked to stealing some money from a charity to fund her university degree. She was working for the charity on a voluntary basis at the time and fully intended to pay the money back. She was caught and endured a publicly humiliating aftermath. She acknowledged feeling guilty about the event and of course apologized, pleading her case. However, her father was a local politician and the conflict within her own mind was part of an ongoing pattern of excessive criticism: you have done wrong, you should suffer. This was her father's influential voice, always in the background, focussed on judgement and what people might think. We worked on helping her unlearn and reframe the situation. She deeply regretted what she had done. It was a misguided decision at a particular moment in time but it didn't deserve eternal self-criticism and self-punishment.

HOW YOU CAN MOVE FORWARD

Earlier I suggested you note down three regrets that trouble you and link them to some unhelpful patterns that you may be able to identify. We will now take this to the next level to help you let go. This will be a three-step process and will include:

1. **Naming and understanding** any regrets that you feel inhibit your life.
2. **Making amends** with others to minimize the power of any unhelpful beliefs surrounding the mistakes.
3. **Forgiving yourself.**

The steps below focus on regrets involving another person or other people but the steps are exactly the same regardless of what the regret is.

STEP 1: NAMING AND UNDERSTANDING

This step involves careful reflection over the period of your entire lifespan, as far back as you can remember. My suggestion is that you reflect on ten-year periods, for example ages one to ten, eleven to twenty, twenty-one to thirty, etc. Using your journal, list the regrets that still bother you in any way. I suggest you write a bullet point summary of all your regrets, then go back and add more information detailing your understanding of why this regret still troubles you. Our work together so far will help with this. Here is a hypothetical example of how you might do this.

Naming regret
I lied to my parents about my exam results when I was sixteen. They were angry and upset when they discovered I'd lied.

Understanding of this regret
My parents held high expectations of me. I thought I had to be perfect and feared their disappointment. I lied to avoid feeling humiliated or to feel like I'd let them down.

Remember this step is not about justifying any wrongdoing. The key aim is to bring the issue to light (shame doesn't do well in light) and understand your own processes better.

Hopefully this example demonstrates that the held regret was a reaction to an underlying belief. In naming and understanding, you then also begin to understand why regret has arisen and lingered longer than needed.

Using the same steps, continue with all of the regrets you have noted, and be aware for each how the event makes you feel. Some events may evoke stronger emotional responses than others, and that is totally normal. Take as much time as you need with this step, and if uncomfortable feelings like guilt, shame, remorse or regret emerge, then be mindful that this is normal. You can decide to acknowledge the feelings but not be overwhelmed by them. This gets easier with practice, I promise.

STEP 2: MAKING AMENDS

This step may not be needed for every mistake in your life. Ultimately, only you can decide which regrets you may need to make amends for. Many twelve-step addiction programmes include 'making amends' for wrongdoing as part of their work. They believe it helps on the road to recovery because making amends from a place of kindness or desire to move forward produces feel-good chemicals such as dopamine and serotonin. We literally feel good when we do something 'good'. It is worth now stopping for a moment to consider a time recently when you did something nice for someone. How did it make you feel? How did the other person respond? Was there a change in your mood? Did you feel better about yourself?

My guess is that your answers will be positive ones. Equally, in deciding to make amends for a regretful action from the past, you also open yourself up to a feel-good response.

It is worth bearing in mind that there is a possibility that the recipient may not want to accept your attempts at making amends (particularly if they have been hurt by you). However, the key thing to remember is that your intentions are coming from a healthy place. If you have tried, then that is enough. If the person or people are unable to accept your attempts at amends now, that's not to say they won't later.

How you make amends, only you can decide. It would be impossible to provide a prescriptive formula, as there are so many variables to consider. It's very much a personal decision.

Nevertheless, these guidelines may be helpful:

- Be clear about your motivation for making amends
- Authenticity – check with yourself that it's coming from a good place
- Seek permission from the aggrieved party to establish contact
- Write an honest letter

- Make appropriate amends (avoid excessive gifts, etc.)
- Offer an explanation for your actions both now and at the time of the mistake
- Be open to the possibility of rejection from the other party
- Never force something that another person is not comfortable with.

When all is said and done making amends is a self-healing process that hopefully translates to the other person, leading to a dual healing process. It is not a selfish act. It is an act of self-care, maturity and it comes from a desire to grow as a human being.

Whatever your desired outcome from making amends, I wish you genuine healing in this important step towards a happier you.

STEP 3: FORGIVING YOURSELF

Forgiveness is a word that is often used out of context and sometimes in an unhelpful 'woolly' way. However, in the context of regret it can't be omitted. If you can't forgive yourself for any wrongdoings or regrets then you will continue to suffer.

I could attempt to offer numerous suggestions on how you forgive yourself but I don't have an answer that will be specific to you. This resolution has to come from you and you will know what action is needed to forgive yourself. The way I view this is that people are highly skilled at punishing themselves. I believe you will inherently know how to forgive yourself. My only suggestion is that self-compassion is at the heart of whatever route you choose. Try to think also of how you would treat another human being who is suffering; now apply that to yourself. The main issue here is not so much how you will forgive, it's making the choice to do so.

I am reminded of an event in my life in relation to forgiveness.

Many years back, as a young Catholic teenager, I went to confession one Saturday afternoon. Let me set the scene for any non-Catholics. Essentially, you go into a dark box, with a priest on the other side of a screen, to confess all of your sins (from a psychological perspective, it's an opportunity to offload any regrets). It's really an act of self-forgiveness but with a rubber stamp from God via a priest! I was in a particularly mischievous stage of my development and I had quite a few regrets to confess! Sometimes there would be a queue of people outside the confession box waiting for atonement, just as one would queue for the January sales hoping for a bargain.

On this particular occasion, the priest on duty was partially deaf. He started the confession by asking me to speak up, as his hearing aid had been left at a wedding reception the day before. Unaware of how loudly I was speaking, I began to confess my list of sins. At the end, I was told to pray a Rosary. Now that's a lot of prayer!

As I left the confession box, I was in a calm state of 'no regret'. My slate had been wiped clean with forgiveness. That didn't last long. I stepped out of the box to find my mum's best friend sitting outside. Well, her face was like thunder as she stood up and started to tut repeatedly like some sort of beat-boxing rapper. I had an immediate urge to run away but I stood frozen. She stared at me and began listing my sins. 'Sexy thoughts, drinking cider and wanting to punch your father . . .' (long pause) 'Does your mother know?' I can remember smirking, thinking of the ABBA song, but this wasn't the time for jokes.

I'd been caught out, shamed, and no number of Rosaries was going to get me out of this one. Full details of my confession were, of course, reported back to my mother and I was reprimanded.

However, my now late mother's response was entertaining. She said that she could understand me wanting to punch my father, she knew most teenagers experimented with drink, but she couldn't believe that I was having sexy thoughts about girls. Was she psychic? A few years later she was going to have her suspicions confirmed!

I think I can safely say that your route to self-forgiveness, whatever you choose, will likely be much more straightforward and won't require a confession box. For the Catholics among you who might opt for confession, check there is no one outside before you start talking!

HOW THIS WILL CONTRIBUTE TO YOUR HAPPINESS

Our brains can at times become cluttered with excess baggage. Regrets take up space. When you spend a lot of time ruminating (going over mistakes again and again), your brain's ability to think clearly is compromised. Let me describe it another way. If the power supply in your home was in a cupboard that was packed with loads of junk, what do you think the problem might be in the event of a power failure? Do you think it would be easy to solve the problem quickly? Do you think it will help you having to battle through lots of junk to get to the source? I'm guessing not.

Maybe a better idea would be to clear out the cupboard of all the stuff that isn't required. Who needs a twenty-year-old ironing board or broken Christmas decorations?

Our brains are like this cupboard. Sometimes we need to de-clutter. There are times in life when we need to function well, such as during difficult circumstances. In times of crisis or distress we may need to access our pre-frontal cortex (the part of the brain that helps us regulate our emotions and think rationally). If our brains are packed with old material like regrets, then our right- and left-brain regulation is out of whack. The result of this is higher anxiety levels and difficulty regulating our moods. In short, there is just too much going on. If a regret has not been dealt with then it may stay active. It will seem as if it's an event that's still happening or has just happened and will occupy your thoughts in the way you'd expect a 'here and now' event to – all the time. This is similar to trauma events. The brain needs to store memories away in an area called the hippocampus (like a library in which memories are filed). Filing memories away and placing them where they belong prevents them from creating current distress in the here and now.

In summary, clearing away some junk and reducing patterns of rumination around regrets will reduce anxiety, improve your mood and your brain function. This will open the way to a more mindful approach to life. Research tells us that a quieter, less cluttered mind equals:

- Increased brain plasticity (more flexibility)
- Increased grey matter in the brain (better memory and concentration)
- A less active threat centre
- Improved creativity
- Improved emotional regulation
- Improved functioning overall.

I hope this convinces you of the value of not holding on to regrets. As humans, we can be our own worst enemies at times.

COMMITMENT

Given that we've evolved to automatically replay our regrets over and over, committing to moving on from our regrets is not an easy task. The truth is we like to punish ourselves. It's a warped part of our make up. The next time you fall into the trap of beating yourself up over an old error maybe it's worth reminding yourself that you are essentially committing an act of self-punishment. The only commitment I am going to ask of you here is to consider an act of self-care instead. This is your commitment at this stage because:

- You don't deserve to continue suffering
- It achieves nothing of value
- It impacts you and those around you negatively
- It gets in the way of you living your life
- You deserve better.

Take a few moments now to write in your journal a personal commitment to yourself on how you will manage the regrets of your life – past, present and whatever is to come. This can be in the form of a letter or note to yourself in which you are clear on your position on whatever regret you are managing. This is something you can go back to at any time if you need a reminder. Trust me, there will be times when you need to revisit this commitment! It is part of your humanity and sometimes we all need to learn how to respond to ourselves in a humane way.

CASE STUDY

This is the story of a professional football player, Joe, who I met on a long-haul flight when he was travelling to meet his team for a game. We got to chat during the flight and our respective careers came up in conversation. I know little about football but enough to get by as my younger brother played professionally.

As the conversation progressed, we developed an affinity with each other. He showed a genuine interest in my work. He clearly was passionate about football, but I could tell from the dips in his vocal tone and dullness in his eyes that there was something missing from his story. It was almost as if he was apologetic about his success. I must confess, I was curious.

Then out of nowhere there was a sudden pause in the conversation and he said, 'I'll never truly win a game.' I asked him what he meant and his story moved me.

He told me that he played in left-back position and had a reputation for setting up goals for other players. But in his teenage years, Joe was involved in an incident involving mechanical equipment at his family home. He'd been messing around with a piece of machinery but had forgotten to switch it off. Moments later his brother had picked up the piece of equipment, thinking it was off. He was left permanently disabled.

Joe hadn't been able to forgive himself for the mistake, so much so that he considered what should have been a positive memory – when a few years earlier he'd scored the winning goal for a tournament, prompting praise from his teammates – as one of the worst moments of his life.

The thought of people cheering and celebrating his successes on the pitch was too much to bear.

Joe's holding on to this regrettable event in his life had stopped him experiencing joy. But it didn't need to be that way. And the same goes for you. You can choose happiness but sometimes that involves having to let go of the things you regret.

SUMMARY

- Regrets are common.
- When you get stuck in a pattern of regret, aim to start letting go.
- Your regrets are fuelled by underlying patterns and beliefs but you can change this.
- Naming, understanding and making amends for regrets will help you heal.
- Self-forgiveness will help you move forward.
- Unresolved regrets will impact upon your happiness if you don't deal with them.

CHAPTER 4

THE WORRY TRAP

'Don't Worry, Be Happy' is one of those songs that sticks in your head, and not just because of the catchy melody! It's also a helpful mantra. If it's still in your mind at the end of the chapter, you will understand my point.

There are vast amounts of research linking worry to mood alterations. Excessive worry makes us unhappy. When we worry less, we are happier. But wouldn't it be great if we could just sing the song and our worries disappeared? Sadly, it isn't that simple!

With that in mind, I couldn't omit worry from a book about how to be happier. Worry, in my view, is one of the modern epidemics. We are

Generation Anxiety and we are worried about many things:

- Our planet
- Our future
- Our income
- Our economy
- Our politics
- Climate change
- Our sea life
- Our bodies
- Our families
- Our safety
- Terrorist activities
- Virus outbreaks
- Our fellow human beings who live in hunger
- Our fellow human beings who are persecuted for their colour, race and sexuality

The list is endless.

It seems the only certainty we have in the world today is that we live in uncertainty and therein lies the problem.

A definition of generalized anxiety disorder describes anxiety as an intolerance of uncertainty. I mentioned earlier that I try to avoid diagnostic labels where possible but this link is important to mention. I am going to assume that most readers of this book have experienced, or will experience, excessive worry at some stage (with or without anxiety disorder labels). If you are living on the same planet as me, it's hard not to!

I am not interested in exploring with you how to get rid of worry. It's not possible. I want to help you manage your relationship with worry. Real changes can happen when this relationship is mastered.

There is an amusing fable of a woman who worried about everything. She would wake up every morning worrying about the day ahead. Throughout the day she would attempt to problem-solve every single concern in her life. One day she was offered the opportunity to meet a guru who promised he could quieten her anxious mind completely. People from all over the world wanted to meet this guru but he was only in the country for one day.

On the day of the meeting, the woman became terribly anxious and informed her husband en route that she didn't want to meet the guru. He was perplexed and couldn't understand why she would want to miss this wonderful opportunity to potentially live worry free.

But she responded, 'I can't go to see this guru

man because who will worry about all these important things I worry about? What will I do with my time?'

And she insisted her husband drive her back home.

When she arrived home, she sat down on her chair and let out a sigh. 'That's better, I've so many things to think about today.'

She was back at home, comfortably uncomfortable with a day of worry ahead.

Do you identify with this? Worry can be almost addictive. It can provide a false sense of security and feel reassuringly familiar.

For many years, I facilitated 'managing worry' groups in my NHS job. I was always struck that at the start of treatment many people became anxious about the treatment itself with a host of common concerns such as:

- What if I miss something I should be worrying about?
- What will I do with my time when I stop worrying?
- What will people think of me if I become different?
- What if people think I don't care about them or things any more?

- What if I lose some of my identity?
- What if something goes wrong that I could have prevented?
- What if I don't want to stop worrying?

It's really interesting for me as a therapist that the worries in themselves, whatever they are, pose less of a challenge than the relationship with worry. There is a habitual keenness to worry sometimes, similar to engaging with an addictive drug, that is hard to stop. It begs the question, have we become hooked on our patterns of worry as a society? Worry has almost become the new norm. Even children are worrying more, with some studies suggesting a 48 per cent increase in anxiety and depression over the past decade.

Yet despite all of this I believe there is a way to let go of habitual, unnecessary worry. I don't promise to eliminate justifiable concerns but I'm confident I can help you rethink your engagement with worry.

Without a doubt, I know worry will be getting in the way of your happiness whether you are aware of it or not. The good news in all of this is that you have a choice about how you manage this part of your life. We'll start with trying to understand why you might be stuck in this pattern of behaviour.

Don't worry, my goal is to help you feel a little happier. Just like the song.

Is the melody still in your head? I told you so.

WHY YOU BECOME STUCK

We all know what worry feels like. Some degree of worry is normal and sometimes worry can be useful in helping us find resolutions to problems in our life. However, when it becomes excessive, that's when issues arise. For me, excessive worry is like an oppressive dark cloud that moves in, hovers around and threatens any peace in my day. It can leave me unsettled and restless. I am keen to push the cloud away as quickly as I can by thinking my way out of it. Yet the harder I try, the worse it gets. I've thankfully learnt ways of managing this and I'll come back to those later.

Before I trained as a therapist I didn't really understand worry. Why is it there? How do I manage it? I wholeheartedly believe that to be able to manage worry you need to understand why you worry. Equally you need to take some responsibility for your role in the process. Now I know this might sound harsh, but it's not. Breakthroughs with worry management come when you acknowledge you have a large part to play.

Someone recently got angry with me on a social media forum when I posted some tips for managing worry. A woman messaged me saying that people with worries or anxieties don't need tips; they need empathy, someone to listen and permission to tell their story – over and over again. I agree empathy and listening are important but without solutions people get stuck in habitual patterns. Encouraging people to ruminate isn't helpful and all the research on anxiety is clear on that. I suspect the person who messaged me was very familiar with her pattern of worry and the thought of change was frightening. My suggestions threatened her way of being, so she decided to fight back.

Isn't it incredible that we sometimes resist suggestions that could help move us forward? I call this the 'comfortably uncomfortable syndrome' and you might experience it when reading this book. It's worth being mindful of this. Happiness isn't fairy dust that falls from the sky, indiscriminately choosing some people and not others; it takes work, commitment and sometimes it involves a lot of letting go.

There will always be things in life to worry about, and the worries will vary depending on the stage of life you're at. I call this the external content.

It's the events, people or circumstances we don't have much control over. For example, as I am writing this book I'm worrying about an ageing dog, an ill father and the prospect of moving house. I'm also getting older and worrying about a receding hairline, my future pension and my increased enjoyment of TV programmes like *Antiques Roadshow*.

In Chapter 2 we discussed disengaging from the content of our minds and learning the skill of observing our thought processes. With worry or anxiety patterns there are specific processes at play that contribute to distressing feelings. It is important to understand what is going on. I'm going to keep this simple. There are two aspects to your worry or anxiety:

1. Your mind and worry.
2. Your relationship with worry.

YOUR MIND AND WORRY

Try to think of your mind like a computer. Sometimes your computer programme gets activated. This sets off a chain of events that automatically generates thoughts, worries, more thoughts and more worries.

Here's how it works:

- The brain's threat system, otherwise known as the amygdala (its fight or flight mechanism that supports you in times of real danger), is overactive in times of imagined danger or threat. For example, you are about to go into a job interview. The threatened feeling this creates will then trigger a series of mental and physical events.
- This stimulates a stress response, which is the release of chemicals such as cortisol and adrenaline.
- The release of hormones causes physical symptoms of stress such as increased blood pressure, increased heart rate, rapid breathing, muscle tension, headaches and dry mouth, among others.
- The mind then begins to create content in the form of worries (which are essentially problem-solving thoughts) as a means of thinking away the fear: protecting you, defending you, keeping you safe. (Your worries actually make the fear worse as the fight or flight response is already on red alert.) Typical thinking could be, What if I forget information? What if they don't like me? What if I freeze?

- The mind recognizes that you are taking its threats seriously and interprets that as the 'danger' still being present, keeping the flight or fight response engaged. This repeating neurological problem is called an anxiety loop.
- Remember, this is an automatic response and it will keep going until you intervene.

To extend the analogy, I think of our brains as running with faulty programming (like a defective computer). The nature of life with its heightened stress, sophisticated development of language and increased pressures means we are operating with a computer (our minds) that has been programmed to be on heightened alert a lot of the time. The problem is, this isn't necessary. If we don't stop to review our programming or reset it then the cycle continues.

So that's the automated mechanics of the mind and how it produces excessive worry.

The second part is your role as the computer programmer inadvertently helping keep this problem alive.

YOUR RELATIONSHIP WITH WORRY

This part is less technical as it's simply about whether you engage with the content of the 'defective' computer programme that's producing excess worry.

The key components keeping this faulty programming running include:

- Telling yourself worry is positive and healthy as a means of preventing harm
- Overthinking
- Seeking solutions by thinking about things repeatedly
- Avoiding things (e.g. I am worried the plane will crash so I will never fly)
- Reassurance-seeking for certainty (my partner didn't text, I need to know they still love me)
- Hyper-vigilance (e.g. if I don't check my child's temperature every day, they may get sick)
- Repeating the same daily pattern with worry.

Unbeknownst to you, by doing the above, you contribute to the endless worry your mind is creating and the cycle continues. You are caught in a cycle of worry that *only you* can break. In psychology these are called safety-seeking behaviours. The irony is, while they may create a degree of short-term reassurance, longer term they keep worry alive and kicking!

As you can see, taking responsibility for your role in all of this is key. A doctor, therapist, friend or anyone else cannot do this work for you (although they can act as a guide). Essentially you are required to create a new computer programme for your mind by breaking these patterns. I will teach you next how to do this.

For now though, I want you to stop and reflect on how much this resonates with you.

Keep a note in your journal of what is relevant for you. What safety-seeking behaviours keep your worries going? Remember that when you are aware you are half way there. Identifying and understanding these issues is an important part of the process.

HOW YOU CAN MOVE FORWARD

By now, you will be aware of why you might be struggling with worry, how the brain influences this and how your safety-seeking behaviours maintain the problem.

It is important to highlight that there isn't an instant solution for this but there are techniques that work. Unhelpful patterns that have been learnt can also be unlearnt. But this takes time, patience and commitment to retraining your brain. You are learning to respond to worry in a different way so it will take practice. Some days will go well, other days will feel like a disaster. The key point to remember is that every conscious effort to change these patterns moves you a step forward.

How you decide to use my suggestions will depend largely on the extent of your worry and your individual patterns. Use whatever works for you and don't feel the need to follow everything prescriptively to the letter.

Here are the steps I suggest you follow (you will need your journal to take notes here):

- Make a list of your top worries.
- Ask yourself the question: Have any of these worries ever come true? Most won't have. However, if the answer is yes to any of the worries, consider changing your thought pattern from *what if*, to *then what*. The shift from *what if* to *then what* is more resolution-focussed and will lead you to think practically about how you will manage a particular situation should something go wrong. It is preferential to powerless entrapment in worry mode. For example, you are due to fly to a friend's wedding and the worry, What if I miss my flight? arises. You have missed a flight previously so this seems a valid worry. When you replace *what if* with *then what* the focus moves away from the worry and towards the solution. If I miss my flight, then I will explore other travel options, I will contact the bridal party to explain the situation and I will focus on finding a way of getting to the wedding. Do you notice the difference?
- Stop and consider whether you view worry as a positive thing and explore with yourself the possibility of dropping this belief.

- Make space for dedicated 'worry time' in your day. This is a dedicated ten minutes every day where you give yourself permission to write down your worries. The benefit of this is that if you get interrupted with worries in your day, you have the option to park them rather than getting derailed. You can return to that worry at a designated time. You may discover your worry has lost its power when you do return to it or you may have forgotten it. This is normally indicative that the worry wasn't warranted in the first place.

Earlier you listed some of the safety-seeking behaviours you participate in that help maintain worry. At this stage the practical challenge is to gradually start to drop some of your safety-seeking behaviours. For example, if you won't go on a train because you worry about an accident, a positive step would be to take a short train journey, even for one stop! This will send a message to the brain that you aren't engaging with the unhelpful worry and new patterns can emerge.

Please be mindful that dropping safety-seeking behaviours will be a challenge. Work at a pace that is comfortable and manageable for you. Sometimes you may need the support of someone close to you and in some cases a professional. A reminder again that you are dropping behaviours because they only give you short-term relief but keep worry alive longer term. You are doing the opposite of what you normally do with worry, so expect discomfort and some doubt. This is normal. Remember, you are developing a new, healthier relationship with your worry which, in the long run, leads to a happier you.

Before closing this section I will summarize how a client of mine used these techniques to help him manage his worry patterns around losing his job.

CASE STUDY

Sammy is a twenty-nine-year-old man, married with two children. His childhood was turbulent and he had numerous foster placements. Stability was lacking for most of his formative years.

He developed acute anxiety and worry patterns around losing his job, all closely attributed to his childhood. As an adult Sammy was happily married and very successful in his job. However, he found his worry hard to control.

In working through the process I have just described, this was how Sammy recovered from his attachment to worry:

- He was able to identify his worries and see they were irrational.
- None of his worries had ever come true.

- He was able to recognize that he viewed worry as a positive thing and decided to drop this as it was impacting on his life negatively.
- Worry time worked well for Sammy and after several weeks he didn't have enough to worry about to fill the ten minutes.
- Sammy's safety-seeking behaviours were looking for constant reassurance from his boss and double-checking all his work. He, in a phased manner, let go of these safety-seeking behaviours and his anxiety reduced.

Sammy's mood improved significantly once his worry was under control. Worrying less helped him achieve a happier life, especially at work.

In summary, Sammy was able to see his relationship with worry was the real problem, not the worry itself. Whatever your worry patterns are, be assured you can regain control. I recommend that you take

> small steps initially with these techniques and in time you will notice major changes. Which leads me on to the benefits of worrying less.

HOW THIS WILL CONTRIBUTE TO YOUR HAPPINESS

Worrying is a normal part of the human condition but excessive worry can lead to more chronic anxiety. Anxiety creates stress and stress impacts detrimentally on our physical and mental wellbeing. Everything eventually interlinks. There are hundreds of articles and research papers reinforcing this and their findings align exactly with my experience of working with worried clients. I'll often see the following changes in my formerly anxious clients once they learn to handle worry:

- Improved mood
- Better health
- Clarity of mind
- Work improvement

- Improved relationships
- Improved concentration
- Openness to healthy risk
- Tolerance of uncertainty
- Better sleep
- More energy

In a nutshell, when you are unburdened from worry, your life becomes lighter in the best possible way. A lighter life is unquestionably a happier life.

One of my favourite scenes is from a movie called *The Mission.* There's a beautiful moment when a character called Mendoza reaches the peak of a mountain he's been climbing with many sacks. He's a troubled character and all the stuff he's carrying serves as a physical representation of his many burdens, his worries and his troubled past. At the top of the mountain a Guaraní man poignantly cuts off Mendoza's sacks and throws them over a cliff, freeing him, cathartically, of all his internal burdens. It is Mendoza's moment of liberation.

Many of us, I believe, are following similar journeys. Life can feel like it's a mountain to climb. We are all carrying excess baggage and our minds are burdened with many worries. Today can be the day when some of those worries can be released and metaphorically thrown over the cliff – just like Mendoza. They hold you back. They don't serve you well.

COMMITMENT

For your commitment in this chapter I have an exercise I suggest you try. I was assigned it many years ago on a meditation retreat and I found it very helpful.

Go back to your list of top worries. Then decide which of these worries you can let go of and write them on a piece of paper. You can let go of your worries in phases if that works better for you.

When you feel ready, light a small fire in a safe outdoor place and burn the list of worries you've decided to let go of. As you watch the flames burn, make a commitment to yourself that from here onwards you won't carry unnecessary worry around with you.

If this exercise doesn't feel right, there are alternative actions:

- Shred the list.
- Place the list in a river or in the sea.
- Erase what you have written.
- Release the list into the sky in a balloon.
- Release the list on a mountain.

Be as creative as you want to be. The research tells us that the action of physically doing something, as opposed to simply making a commitment in your mind, can help set up new, better patterns.

However you decide to commit to this part of your life, you will find a new lightness and freedom, unquestionably.

WAKE-UP CALL: PERSPECTIVE ON WORRY FROM THE DYING

As I've mentioned, the early years of my career were spent working in the field of palliative care, supporting people living with terminal illness. Those in my care ranged in age from seventeen to over ninety.

Many of the clients had not expected a terminal illness diagnosis so you can imagine the psychological journey this often led them on. Amidst initial angst, heartache, fear, and confusion, often I would observe wisdom emerge. It was as if dying, for some, opened up new possibilities for living. All the 'stuff' we usually worry about seemed less important and often I would hear clients describe worry as almost futile.

It is almost impossible to work in this area and not change in some way. I'd often feel a little embarrassed arriving at work with my list of worries percolating in my mind: What's the best mortgage deal? Where shall I go on holiday? Why hasn't my partner called me back?

And then I would sit at the bedside of a twenty-five-year-old man dying of cancer telling me how happy he is because his consultant has approved his request to go on a fishing trip that weekend. Later a young mother of three children tells me how grateful she is because she managed to spend Christmas with her kids after all. Yes, I would leave work feeling a mix of challenged, uneasy, inspired and deeply respectful of the perspective some of these people had.

Worry often wasn't prioritized or given much airtime and that made the transition at the end of life easier.

For those clients who did worry, the worries were often real, valid and needed some support.

I know you may very well have worries that are real, valid and require your focus.

And I don't wish to minimize that in any way. But we do need to recognize the many additional worries that we create and unnecessarily entertain. When we do this, we sabotage our personal happiness.

I want to end this section on worry with a conversation I had with a guy called Mike, aged forty-one, who had just been told a week prior that he had three months to live. He was very withdrawn but pensive when I sat down with him. I assumed he was anxious about his diagnosis and everything that entailed. As any clinician would do, I started to explore with him what was on his mind. In truth, I had a list of assumptions about what his worries might be (having worked in the field for a while) but he surprised me.

I asked Mike if there was anything specifically troubling him that day. He went quiet for a moment then responded, 'I'm just trying to work out how I make the best of the next three months.'

I think it says it all really. Worry will sabotage your happiness if you don't take a step back and regain some control.

I hope that as you reflect on your relationship with worry, some of these lessons encourage you to opt for making the best of your time on this planet. When we worry less, we live more. When we live more, we tend to be happier. You are not your thoughts. You are so much more.

> ### SUMMARY
>
> - Worry is a normal part of the human experience.
> - Excessive habitual patterns of worry contribute to anxiety.
> - Understanding how your mind works will help you regain a sense of control.
> - The problem is often your relationship with worry rather than the worries themselves.
> - Change *what if* to *then what* thinking.
> - Create a dedicated 'worry time' to prevent worrying from derailing your day.
> - Less worry contributes to a happier life.
> - Remind yourself that you are not your thoughts.

CHAPTER 5

HELL IS OTHER PEOPLE

As a therapist, I hear many parents express concerns that their children will 'fall in with the wrong crowd'. They worry that negative influences will impact the child's future and potential to succeed. In fairness, this may be a warranted concern. Children don't always have the capacity to make wise decisions on the positive influencers in their life. They, mostly, want to fit in, belong and have some degree of popularity. Children also don't have the emotional maturity, insight and years of life experience that adults have. So, undoubtedly, they will make mistakes and sometimes choose unhealthy friendships, role models or heroes. As they grow older they will learn from their errors and make healthier choices, which contribute to a balanced, happier life. Or do they?

Well, in short, many do but some don't. One of the obstacles to happiness I witness with the adults I treat is the negative impact of other people in their lives and this can be anyone!

Interestingly, regardless of the relationship, the specific issues people have with problematic individuals in their lives are very similar:

- Dissatisfaction
- Anger
- Conflict
- Distress
- Poor communication
- Blaming
- Isolation
- Loneliness
- Destructive arguments
- Negative behaviours.

In emotional terms this is often expressed as 'I'm feeling . . .

- Undervalued
- Disrespected

- Taken for granted
- Ignored
- Intimidated
- Lesser
- Patronized
- Bullied
- Frightened
- Invisible.'

Of course, this can vary according to circumstance and the nature of the relationship, but in essence, the experience is negatively charged. Consequently, personal happiness is compromised.

The infamous philosopher Sartre once described hell as other people. Let's be honest, he had a point! We all have people in our lives that may create or have created some sort of hell for us.

Perhaps I should rephrase that.

We all have people in our lives we have *allowed* to create hell for us. Yes, that's what's interesting here, for we do in fact have a choice as adults in how we respond to other people. We're no longer children and aren't powerless any more. That said, there are times, in more extreme circumstances, when we might need a little support.

I imagine you may be thinking at this point about the people in your life that have a non-negotiable presence who you don't feel enhance your life in any way. This may include:

- Birth family
- Work colleagues
- Neighbours
- People you share everyday public services with
- People from your past
- In-laws.

However, the good news is, you have a choice in what you will tolerate from other people. You can choose to leave situations that upset you or make you feel uncomfortable. You can create distance between yourself and the difficult people in your life. You can decide how you will respond to the actions of others and limit their impact on how you feel. Yes, you have an absolute right to expect reasonable, decent behaviour from the people in your life. Now, let me be clear, that doesn't mean they will be able to deliver. However, it does mean you have a choice in what you will put up with. That is within your power. You can decide to place boundaries upon the people creating obstacles to your personal happiness. That could include how much time you spend with them, knowing when to walk away or setting up clear expectations of what you will or won't accept.

A few years back I visited South Africa. I had the privilege of visiting Robben Island, one of the prisons Nelson Mandela was incarcerated in for twenty-seven years. On the day of the visit, a former cell mate of Mandela was the tour guide. I had the opportunity to speak to him personally and ask how he survived such a harrowing ordeal. Interestingly he described how the influence of Mandela and a few others had made everything much more bearable. He also commented that the experience would have been so much worse if negative people had surrounded him.

I was really struck by his comments as he focussed more on the people around him, not the adverse circumstances in prison. 'Freedom' was found in the people.

It's the same with those of us who aren't imprisoned! People can truly enrich our lives. But we need to be equally mindful that the opposite happens when we allow ourselves exposure to other people's poor behaviour or negative attitudes.

Maybe now is an appropriate moment to stop and reflect on the relationships or people in your life. Who impacts on your life in a negative way?

At this stage I suggest you list these people and

how they impact on you. Keep it factual, and notice if your tendency is to want to judge or blame them. I encourage you to avoid this. The reasons for this will become clearer later in the chapter.

So let's make more sense of what might be going on here.

WHY YOU BECOME STUCK

Understanding why other people's behaviour impacts on your life is important. It helps you regain a sense of control and gives you an understanding of what you can do to minimize the effects of their behaviour. In my experience, it's helpful to think about what's going on for the other 'difficult' person, as well as your own reaction to them.

The harsh reality is that you are unlikely to fundamentally change another person's behaviour in general. People tend not to change until they are ready, if at all! That said, you can adjust how they behave *towards you* through your responses and by making it clear what you will or won't tolerate. For example, a client of mine recently discussed creating a boundary with a friend who was repeatedly very late for social events. She created a new rule that she wouldn't wait around unless it was a dire emergency.

What follows are some common scenarios of what might be going on when a person takes out their negative emotions on someone close to them (you, in this instance!). You may recognize patterns that mirror particular relationships in your life. Even if these emotional templates aren't completely spot on, they will offer some insight into potential underlying patterns.

- **Transference.** Sometimes people find it hard to acknowledge feelings that belong to them, so they may place them onto you. For example, if someone has experienced abandonment in childhood, they may be easily triggered into experiencing those feelings again. They may misinterpret your actions as abandonment of them and react accordingly – with hurt, blame and accusations.
- **Envious attack.** If a person feels insecure or inadequate they may manage this by launching an envious attack on you. This often translates as judgement, undermining, criticism, gossip or patterns of envy.

- **Aggression.** If emotions are not processed or regulated correctly, the other person may manage these feelings by acting out with aggressive or angry outbursts.
- **Avoidance.** When people find it difficult to deal with issues, they can sometimes become avoidant. This can translate to ignoring you, withdrawing from you or showing unreliability.
- **Low self-worth.** A person who is not feeling good about themselves will sometimes behave negatively or critically towards you to help them manage their own sense of inadequacy.
- **Depression/anxiety.** It is not uncommon for someone who is anxious or depressed to demonstrate changes in behaviour such as irritability, lack of interest, low motivation or generalized anger.

There are other negative behaviour patterns, some of which could fill an entire book in themselves, but the main thing to acknowledge is that however another person is behaving, they are likely suffering. This knowledge will help you when we look at how to manage people.

WHAT'S GOING ON WITH YOU?

Before looking at what techniques you can use when dealing with negative behaviours from others, I am going to assume one thing: you are tolerating these behaviours towards you – in other words, you are *allowing* them. The reality is, we all do. But why do we tolerate this? Well, apart from some of the obvious reasons such as love, duty or lack of choice, there are likely more complex processes and patterns at play:

- **Passivity.** A sense of powerlessness over others' behaviour results in you accepting it and feeling very dissatisfied.
- **Fear of conflict.** Often you may feel it's easier to pacify others rather than deal with their bad behaviour, but in the long run this leads to more problems.
- **Low self-worth.** Doubting whether you deserve to be treated well and respectfully.
- **People pleasing.** You may have a fear of saying no to people or challenging others, linked to a fear they will reject you.
- **Loneliness.** Worry that the loss of a relationship will lead to isolation or loneliness, which might feel intolerable for you.

- **Unhealthy patterns.** Sometimes poor behaviours are tolerated and normalized as 'OK' and may have become part of a habitual cycle for you.
- **Learnt behaviours.** If you have witnessed others tolerating poor behaviours, for example, within the family, then it's possible you may repeat the same patterns.

Whatever process goes on for you, the reality is that when people behave badly towards you, it's not a nice experience. You are left with a host of residual negative feelings from your interactions with them that don't necessarily belong to you. Essentially they have displaced their feelings onto you. It is reasonable to point this out to the person and explain that whilst you are keen to support them, they need to manage some of these feelings better.

As I am writing this section I am reminded of an incident in the early days of my hospital career. I was part of a 'ward round' (when a team of health professionals visit clients and plan care) in a busy hospital. The lead clinician on this particular occasion asked each team member to contribute suggestions or insights into patient care. I noticed on a few occasions the clinician was sharp and a little rude to other colleagues. As the afternoon progressed, the situation worsened. It all came to a head when I was asked to justify my reasoning for prescribing a particular anti-sickness drug to a patient.

My drug of choice wasn't standard (but of course within licence) but I had valid reasons for prescribing it: the patient was taking another medication that interacted with the 'usual' medication. As I started to introduce my patient, the lead clinician started to speak over me, shouting repeatedly, 'Wrong, wrong, wrong.' I tried interjecting a few times but was cut short. Later, the clinician started to mock me in an attempt to raise laughter from the rest of my colleagues. When no one laughed I had the opportunity to respond.

In a calm, diplomatic tone, I explained to him that I was offended by the way he was speaking to me. I needed him to listen to my rationale for my treatment choice.

I also added that if he continued to speak over me or mock me, then I wouldn't be able to continue participating in the ward round.

The atmosphere instantly changed. Sheepishly he backed off and I was invited to explain my choice. Later in the day an apology came.

My decision to place clear boundaries on the

clinician, although uncomfortable for me, was the right one, both professionally and personally. If I had not tackled this behaviour, then I would have been allowing my old patterns of passivity and people-pleasing to play out. My decision was to acknowledge these patterns but not allow them to dictate my response.

In terms of the lead clinician, he had displayed aggression and transference in his behaviour. I know this as I discovered later he was managing some very difficult personal circumstances in his own life. The ward round became a time for him to act out his anger and frustration.

But this was not my stuff. The real issue was the clinician's behaviour. Challenging these behaviours was the appropriate thing to do. I would have been disrespecting myself if I had allowed the behaviour to continue. Secondly, the lead clinician likely needed a wake-up call that this wasn't acceptable.

These moments when we challenge, put boundaries in place or resist poor behaviour from others are never easy. Often you will not have the luxury of knowing what is going on for the other person but you can always assume they are suffering at some level. This compassionate approach will benefit you both.

Learning *how* to respond to difficult people in your life is liberating all round.

But a considered, measured response is essential. Any interaction where you're coming into conflict with people will always evoke a series of emotions. Heightened emotions don't normally support rational thinking, which is an essential ingredient for resolution. Letting go of the behaviours of difficult people therefore starts with you.

HOW YOU CAN MOVE FORWARD

It may sound odd or a little unfair that the onus of managing difficult people is on you, but the reality is there will always be challenging people around. If learning how to manage such people enhances your life, then surely it's a worthwhile skill? It can be empowering and gives you a greater sense of control. Remember, you can change your response to challenging people but it's less likely you will ever be able to fundamentally change them.

I have developed four steps that will guide you through the process. The principles are the same regardless of the nature of the relationship:

1. Dialling down your emotional response
2. Pattern recognition and letting go
3. Rational communication
4. Future boundaries.

DIALLING DOWN YOUR EMOTIONAL RESPONSE

We all know that feeling when someone has upset us by his or her actions or words. It can feel like an emotional hurricane. One moment we feel calm and then suddenly we feel rage, or so much hurt.

The issue is that if you respond while in the eye of the storm, you will likely move from a category 3 to category 5 very quickly. The situation then tends to deteriorate with two people (or more if in a group) emotionally aggravated.

Heightened emotions tend to come about very rapidly. However, recognition and understanding of your emotions helps you regain a sense of control, as does learning the skill of managing your emotions. I should preface this by saying that this requires practice. But like every change that you're working to bring about in your psychological patterns, once your brain recognizes that you're responding differently, you will start establishing new neuropathways. This leads to healthier responses.

Here are the steps that will help you reduce your emotional response:

1. Stop and recognize you have been triggered by someone's behaviours.
2. Make a decision that you will take two minutes out and won't respond until you feel emotionally more 'level'. This may involve delaying interaction with the other person, excusing yourself from the situation or taking extra time out. It all depends on the context.
3. During the time out use your breath to slow down both physiological and emotional responses. Breathe in for a count of four and out for a count of four (doing five repetitions). Then allow yourself to be present with your emotions, whatever they are, in a compassionate, understanding manner. Try to avoid overthinking details of the event.
4. Do not engage in any conflict or discussion while the dial on your emotional barometer is high (you will intuitively know what a comfortable level is for you). I think of my emotional barometer as having a scale of one to ten (one being low emotional arousal, ten being high). I never respond when my emotions are five or above.

PATTERN RECOGNITION AND LETTING GO

This process is twofold involving you and the other person. Starting with you, firstly, recognize how you are feeling. For example, your partner may have criticized you in front of the children. How are you feeling?

Record what patterns arise that prevent you from challenging your partner's behaviour. Flick back to the What's going on with you? section (see pages 121–2) for help here.

It could be that the feeling is humiliation and your pattern is passivity to avoid conflict.

The next step would then be to decide that you will let that unhelpful pattern go. In this example, you might decide that you won't allow yourself to be humiliated and, instead of passivity, you might opt for assertiveness. I will explore later how to communicate this effectively.

Now focus on the other person. Consider what might be going on for them. As we have discussed, we can't fully know the circumstances of the other person but we can assume they are potentially suffering in some way.

In this example, the partner who's criticizing may be feeling inadequate as a parent. She or he manages this by using a pattern of transference resulting in them criticizing and humiliating their partner. They need to know that this is their 'stuff' and that treating their partner in this way is not acceptable or healthy. Challenging their behaviour might help them see this.

RATIONAL COMMUNICATION

Arguments or disagreements worsen when communication is poor. In this step, you will now be approaching the situation with a calmer perspective following the preparation you've done. You will have taken time out to dial down your emotional response and recognized the activated patterns that prevent you from challenging bad behaviour and therefore need releasing. Now you will communicate clearly, openly and honestly what you feel.

The key points to remember here are:

- Stick to the facts and a non-blaming tone, i.e. being objective rather than emotive. For example, imagine you have a disagreement with a friend who has cancelled dinner with you on two consecutive occasions. In this instance, rather than blame or get angry, you explain factually what has happened and how it leaves you feeling.
- Express how the situation made you feel.
- If interrupted, insist you are properly heard.
- Be clear that you won't tolerate future similar behaviours or actions.
- Show compassion when the other person expresses vulnerability or remorse.
- If the situation deteriorates further, be prepared to walk away and be clear that you won't return to the conversation until the situation is calmer.

Remember one calm person in a conflict is significantly more likely to restore equilibrium than two distressed people.

FUTURE BOUNDARIES

It is pointless trying to resolve issues with the challenging people in our life unless we are crystal clear about what we will and won't tolerate. Without these boundaries people can sometimes run riot with how they treat us.

For example, if you're in a relationship that is in any way abusive, violent or manipulative then you might need to seek help to support how you manage the situation, especially if you are at any risk. There are many professional organizations out there who offer support in times of need or crisis (I have provided a list at the end of the book).

My suggestion at this stage is that you go back to your list of unhealthy relationships or people. For each one, consider what your new boundaries will be. You'll immediately feel liberated.

When you are clear about what you want or expect, others will be clearer on what your expectations are. They may not like it but your purpose in life is not to please everyone. However, do be realistic. Having super-high expectations of people will mean you set yourself up for a fall.

My final point may be worth pondering for a moment. Who are your 'tribe' in life? Are you surrounding yourself with positive, uplifting people who 'get' you? Sometimes we fall into tribes or sub-tribes where we don't belong. That can be an uncomfortable way to live and it doesn't contribute to happiness. But you *can* move on from relationships that are holding you back or not serving you well. It won't be easy. Moving on from unhealthy relationships can be tough as they are often long-standing and familiar. But in the long run, they create potential for more hurt. And remember in the future to choose your tribes carefully. Always be aware that if they don't value you or treat you respectfully, then they are not your tribe.

HOW THIS WILL CONTRIBUTE TO YOUR HAPPINESS

People are energy forces. We feel people's energy when we're around them. Next time you are with someone you admire, respect and feel energized by, note how his or her energy makes you feel. These people are normally quite magnetic personalities. The essence of such people can be contagious, leaving you feeling renewed. Outside of the world of psychology and neuroscience, new age theories describe this as a person's aura. While difficult to quantify scientifically, at an experiential level, I think there is much truth in this. We're talking about the same thing when we describe atmospheres at parties or events.

On the other hand, compare this to some you know who have the opposite effect on you. Next time you are with someone that you feel burdened by, note how his or her energy makes you feel. These people normally complain a lot, they use negatively charged language, and they tend to see the worst in people, situations and life. Rather than leaving you energized, they tend to leave you feeling drained, depleted and under-energized.

I notice this every time I go to present to groups or teams of people. Before I speak, I read the energy in the room. Group energy is also contagious and it's tangible when you enter a room.

The following examples of positive emotional responses to other people demonstrate the necessity of being aware of the choices you make regarding the individuals in your life. They're also helpful when you're considering who you might need to place boundaries upon or possibly let go of. With the right people in your life you will notice that:

- You feel energized by the energy they emit.
- Your outlook is optimistic.

- You feel a sense of security from the reassurance they provide.
- Your perspective is more flexible as they influence and encourage you.
- Your confidence will improve from the affirmations they provide.
- You will feel encouraged and inspired by the support they give you.
- You will trust more from the safety they provide.
- You will take more healthy risks as they express their belief in you.
- You will value yourself more because of the respect they show you.
- You will feel better about life because these people are a life force.

Who wouldn't want these benefits?

I challenge you to really stop and consider whether the people in your life at the moment make you feel the benefits I have described. I appreciate none of us can have a completely perfect circle of family and friends. That's not how life works. But you need some energizing life forces. Without these people, happiness is compromised.

Perhaps you owe it to yourself to truly explore this and make the necessary changes. I won't deny this can be tough, but most worthwhile changes aren't easy. Stay focussed on the benefits.

COMMITMENT

It is worth clarifying that I am not suggesting a complete cull of the negative people in your life. As I mentioned earlier some people might simply need boundaries placed around them, some you might need to pull away from for a time and others you truly might need to consider letting go of permanently, in the most compassionate way possible. I know this might sound tough but think of it another way. If people are allowed to behave badly unchallenged, they will continue to act out. I'm not saying they will change fundamentally. They most likely won't. But they will be aware of what you will tolerate and that may alter how they behave around you. You might actually be doing them, as well as you, a favour.

It's down to you how you manage these relationships, the timescales you place upon them and what methods you use to make the necessary changes. It would be wrong for me to try to deliver a one size fits all remedy for this. Relationships can have complex dynamics. However, I refer you to the communication section of this chapter (see pages 129–30), which will be a helpful navigator. Keep in mind that if you attack or reject another, they will fight back. If you reasonably and kindly explain your concerns and what you won't tolerate, it might just sow a seed of change for them.

In your journal now, start to make a few notes planning out your strategy for managing the challenging relationships in your life. If it's impacting your happiness, you can't ignore it.

I believe the people in our lives are often a mirror of how we see ourselves. If you are serious about walking the path of a happier life, you have to be honest with yourself about the quality of the people you allow in. Let the people in your life mirror the better version of you, the happier version of you.

CASE STUDY

I think it's important I share some of my own truth – with my clients and with you – and demonstrate that I've used these techniques myself to tackle my own issues.

I once shared with a patient struggling with grief that I understood her wanting to scream at the world. I felt that way in the depths of my own grief when I lost my mum when she was just fifty-seven. How was that fair or right? Why was a good person taken so young? Where was the God she believed in as she lay in bed crying with pain from cancer? These were my thoughts and I did want to scream 'F*ck off!' every time someone offered a well-meaning platitude like 'She's in a better place now.' Of course, I didn't go into this detail with the patient but she smiled when I identified with her feelings and said, 'It's nice to know you're human!'

And human I am, particularly when it comes to recognizing that other people can get in the way of happiness.

I grew up in Northern Ireland during The Troubles in a working-class area of Belfast called Ardoyne. It was a terrifying place at that time with constant bombs, shootings, killings and fear in the air. It was also a place of love and kindness, which I think was a saving grace for many.

As mentioned at the start of the book, my early life had a few challenges. I was also a 'different' kind of boy. I was a skinny lad with a high-pitched voice who played piano and was more comfortable playing with the girls and telling them how much I liked their pretty hair. I think you get the picture.

My mum told me not to worry and that I was 'special'. As I approached my teenage years, I, of course, knew that 'special' meant gay but I was living in a very male-dominated, heteronormative and intolerant environment. I once had a friend tell me as a teenager that he wanted to be my friend but he would prefer it be secret so the other kids wouldn't laugh at him. There were the beginnings of a sense of shame, humiliation and a concern I wasn't enough.

I soon started to notice that I was grateful when people became my friend because I was frightened people wouldn't want to be seen with the skinny gay kid (who also played the piano).

Fast-forward to my adult years when I had my first experience of therapy (essential as part of a therapist's training). It is here I realized that I had some unhealthy relationships in my life that needed to change.

I noticed people in my life who were sometimes controlling, manipulative and self-serving. They were very happy when I was the submissive and reliable friend. And the truth is, I was that person because I was grateful to have friends. My fear of loneliness or being rejected fuelled that pattern.

As my emotional intelligence has developed over the years, I have learnt to place boundaries, pull back and sometimes let go of relationships that get in the way of my wellbeing and happiness. I now realize that I don't need to be grateful for healthy relationships; I am deserving of them.

The skinny, gay boy who was often the brunt of laughter, taunts and humiliation was actually a creative, kind human being who deserved to be celebrated. As an adult, I learnt my mum was right in identifying my 'specialness' (my sexuality) and that it could be embraced, as could I.

What I realized above everything was that when I allowed the wrong people a place in my life, it never felt comfortable. The friend I would meet for coffee (but feel anxious before meeting them) eventually turned out to be an unhealthy relationship.

I have learnt that if a partner, friend or family member can't support you and pick you up when you're in a dark period, then they do not deserve to take a place in the inner circle of your world.

No relationship is ever perfect. We will all fall short and get it wrong sometimes. But if you have people in your life that consistently let you down, undermine you and don't value you, then why are you allowing that? Is their behaviour impacting upon your self-worth? Is that contributing to your happiness? Only you can decide this.

I leave you with one final thought. The day I realized I was deserving of happiness was the day I allowed myself to be open to it. It was also the day I realized what type of people were blocking my happiness. That was something I had to take responsibility for. I suspect it may be the same for you.

SUMMARY

- The people in your life impact on your happiness.
- It is important to understand that other people's behaviours often have nothing to do with you.
- It is important to understand why you tolerate bad behaviours and be aware of what's right for you and what is not.
- Managing unhealthy relationships is a four-step process of: lowering the emotional barometer, pattern recognition and letting go, rational communication and future boundaries.
- Who you surround yourself with is a reflection of how you see yourself. Make choices that enrich your life and contribute to your happiness.

CHAPTER 6

KICK THE HABIT

Sometimes in life, there's a lot going on. You know how it is. There are a hundred and one things to do but not enough hours in the day.

On top of that, there's no sugar-coating the fact that we live in difficult times. Happiness might feel like it's a delusional goal right now. I understand that. Numerous studies highlight that people feel overwhelmed *a lot* of the time. Next time you're in a busy shopping area or on a crowded train, look at people's expressions. It is a scene of angst, stress and disconnection.

Not to mention that every moment of every day

there are the challenges of your external world (responsibilities, commitments, uncertainty, stressors) as well as your internal world (saboteur, worry, your mind, emotions).

It's no wonder we feel anxious!

Alongside the demands of life, you may also have times when you don't feel great about yourself. I think we can all identify a time in recent memory when our internal saboteur has plagued us with confidence-busting questions such as, Am I good enough? Can I do this? Will I fail? Am I going to make a fool of myself? This voice isn't easy to listen to and it might seem easier to block out your saboteur with external stimuli or 'rewards' such as a new pair of trainers or games on your phone. When the going gets tough it's normal to crave some relaxation, and create distractions to get away from it all.

I occasionally feel overwhelmed, and when I do, a sugar fix or online shopping creates a welcome distraction. And it can be healthy to stop, step back from everyday life and recharge your batteries. Seeking fun, excitement, distraction, achievements or stimuli can feel good. If managed sensibly, they can all be helpful strategies contributing to a sense of balance. So don't worry, I haven't joined the misery police!

Although this behaviour is totally valid and can be healthy, I do have a cautionary message in this chapter, based on many years of experience working on the frontline of physical and mental health services: we should be aware that these distractions *can* become unhealthy habits, which is when they start interfering with other parts of your life, and that's when problems arise.

ARE YOU OVER-RELIANT ON SOMETHING THAT HELPS YOU MANAGE?

Sometimes habits that help manage stressors or emotions become excessive or heavily relied upon. This can lead to other problems such as addiction. This chapter isn't about addiction but it will explore whether you are heavily reliant on habits to cope with your life. The question of whether you are addicted to something or not, only you can answer. There are various theories on addiction or dependency that I won't get into here. But, for simplicity's sake, I think it's safe to say that if you can't function without something or stop doing it when you want to or are required to, then chances are you've become 'hooked' or are over-reliant on it. In this chapter, I'm going to use the expression 'hooked' loosely and you can decide whether it applies to you in any capacity. You may want to use a scale of one to ten (ten being I can't stop it, one being I rarely need it) to help you decide. You may not need to totally abstain from a habit but only you can evaluate what will be most helpful. I would say a regular score above five or six is worth reviewing.

The habits that you think are making you happy can, in the long term, have the opposite effect. Precisely how will become clearer later in the chapter.

Try to keep an open mind with the message I offer in this chapter. Some of what I say here might make you feel a little uncomfortable. I'll be suggesting reducing or taking away some of your 'crutches' (your habits) and you may not like that. Remember, I'm working with you, not against you, with the ultimate goal of removing some of the blocks to your happiness. I'll also be encouraging you to look at replacing some of your unhealthy coping mechanisms with healthier habits.

An important starting point is recognizing what your unhelpful habits might be. These are the activities that impact negatively upon the below aspects of your life, and they need your attention:

- Your mood
- Your health
- Your finances
- Your family
- Your relationships
- Your work life
- Your choices
- Your sleep
- Your motivation
- Your self-worth.

Often, we perform our habits so automatically that they're difficult to identify as problematic.

I can imagine there might be a few things going on in your mind at the moment. You might be wondering what your habits are. You might *know* what they are but feel uncomfortable thinking about them. You might even want to put the book down as thinking about this has suddenly made you feel uneasy.

Whatever you're feeling, I encourage you to hang around as there will unquestionably be something that could help you here. What makes us uncomfortable often makes us grow. A tough pill to swallow, I know, but true.

In my thirty years of working with people who are struggling, I've witnessed that unhealthy habits tend to fall into one of ten patterns:

- Alcohol
- Drugs (prescription and recreational)
- Sex
- Porn
- Shopping
- Gambling
- Food
- Gaming
- Social media
- Achievements such as money, success, power, status, titles and fame.

In line with previous chapters, try to identify which pattern or patterns your unhelpful habits fall into. There are no right or wrong answers here and it doesn't matter if you identify with one pattern or all of them. Try not to judge yourself harshly here. It's tough enough having a saboteur to deal with without giving yourself a hard time too!

Write down in your journal which behaviour patterns you identify with and if you have a few, perhaps prioritize which you'd like to work on first. For now, you are simply identifying and prioritizing.

As we move through the chapter, there will be guidance on how you start to let go of these unhelpful patterns, whatever they are.

I treated a young guy a few years back who was addicted to heroin. He told me he was making good progress and was ready to end therapy – after four sessions! He said he didn't need the 'gear' any more. I could have told myself that I was an amazing therapist, curing this guy in four weeks, but I knew he was having me on! The one thing I should say about my job is that BS-detection comes with the territory, and my detector has become particularly finely honed (if I do say so myself!) following years of practice. I knew he wasn't being honest with himself or me. Upon further enquiry, I discovered he had indeed stopped using heroin but had started using cocaine regularly instead (which he saw as less of a problem). One habit had replaced another.

Sometimes we all tell ourselves the story we want to hear. When it comes to letting go of unhelpful habits, the one thing I require of you above all is brutal honesty with yourself; that's the only way you're going to move forward.

WHY YOU BECOME STUCK

There are three reasons why you might rely on unhelpful habits:

1. You have easy access to quick fixes that feed your habit and make you feel better for a while, for example, alcohol.
2. You have never learnt to self-soothe (self-soothing in this context means to acknowledge your emotions and respond in a non-judgemental way, to make positive self-care choices, regulate your emotions and to be kind to yourself). There will be more on this later in the chapter.
3. You may be in self-destruct mode.

QUICK-FIX HABITS

From the introduction, you will remember that I mentioned the three systems that we operate from as human beings, especially when we are under pressure: threat, drive and soothe. For example, if you are hyper-vigilant, constantly worrying or employing habits that enable you to stay in control, then your threat system is in overdrive. If you're always striving to achieve more or seeking distraction via stimuli such as drugs, then you are operating from drive mode. If you have a balanced lifestyle involving self-care, then you are operating in the healthy soothe mode. In summary, our habits are linked with whatever systems we tend to utilize most. It won't come as a surprise to you that most people are only ever operating from either their threat or their drive systems at any given time. Sadly, the healthier alternative – our soothing system – seems to always be the bridesmaid, never the bride. All systems perform a helpful function when balanced but mental distress occurs when that balance is absent.

Using unhelpful habits to comfort or distract is totally understandable. We are, after all, in the era of instant gratification. We also don't like 'feeling' too much. For example, take Jimmy, a client of mine. His marriage was in difficulty and he was under immense pressure at work. He regularly finished work late trying to catch up and ended the day drinking lots of alcohol. He'd get some short-term relief from his problems by making these choices but the next day he'd struggle because this had been his pattern for several months. He'd feel tired, hungover, irritated, ashamed and ultimately his happiness was compromised.

He used his drive system to engage the habits of over-working and drinking to manage difficult emotions linked to the external world (stress, uncertainty, pressure, unpredictability) as well as internal struggles (such as, Am I enough?). It's not surprising that he'd reach for the bottle as a distraction to soothe and anaesthetize himself, and that others in his situation might do the same.

YOUR SELF-SOOTHE SYSTEM

If Jimmy had opted for his self-soothe mechanism instead when dealing with his marriage crisis and stresses at work, he may have taken a different route. He could have chosen to seek marriage guidance, join a gym or a club, regulate his work hours, seek help with his stress and generally find ways of taking care of himself. He didn't because he didn't know how to and this is often the case.

It is possible you may never have been taught to self-soothe. Let's be honest, these skills are rarely taught at home or school. Many of us have been taught the 'pull yourself together' method. If you haven't learnt about self-soothing or were unaware that it's an option, then is it any wonder you've never used it?

Well, now you can, and I will be teaching you

later how you can activate your amazing self-soothing system.

Remember, it's not just what you didn't learn, it's also what you witnessed or experienced. If you witnessed your family or influential others using unhelpful habits as a way of coping, then chances are you'll do the same. Another reason to stop self-judgement in its tracks as it's simply an unhelpful learnt response.

SELF-DESTRUCTIVE BEHAVIOUR

I see self-destructive behaviour regularly as a therapist. Even when clients discover they have options to manage their lives in a better way, they often continue with the exact same unhealthy habits. This is usually accompanied by a host of excuses as to why things can't improve. Eventually it becomes clear that the habits, whatever they are, come from a drive to self-destruct or from a place of self-loathing. When this happens, the shame that often accompanies these self-destructive behaviours needs to be addressed. Ironically it's often a sense of shame that leads to the behaviours in the first instance, so it a self-perpetuating cycle. If this resonates with you, it's important to remember that only *you* can change this. When your habits are having a destructive, harmful impact on your life, I encourage you to ask yourself *why* you continue to inflict this harm upon yourself? Have you ever considered that you deserve better than this? If you've never asked yourself this question, then perhaps stop for a few moments now and do so.

HOW YOU CAN MOVE FORWARD

I use an eight-step approach for this and I suggest you use it too, and in whatever order works for you:

- Admit there's a problem
- Remind yourself that you're enough
- Create healthier surroundings
- Wean yourself off your habit
- Learn to self-soothe
- Adopt healthier habits
- Identify the support you need to kick your unhealthy habit for good
- Allow for bad days.

At this stage, you should have identified the habits you want to work on. I don't think it's sensible to work on too many areas at one time, so let's start with one and build up to the others.

ADMIT THERE'S A PROBLEM

I can't stress enough how important it is to acknowledge and admit to yourself if you are struggling with an unhealthy habit or addiction. Let me reiterate again what a problematic habit is: it is a behaviour or thought process you perform repeatedly as a means of distraction, or to alleviate stress or anxiety, which comes with a price tag to other areas of your life. I have seen countless people come to my office accompanied by a loved one. Once the therapy door is closed (whilst the loved one waits outside), the client then reports they are fine. They go on to explain they are reassuring their loved one, and then normally attempt to collude with me at some level. Of course, I don't. My normal tactic is to send the person away and suggest they come back when they are ready for help.

To change any habits that don't work for your life, you first have to be able to recognize them as a problem for you. If you are unable to do that, nothing will change. You will not work on changing something that you don't identify as a problem because your intention will lack motivation and desire. That's why honest self-analysis is so important here. Here are some of the lies your denial might feed you at this point:

- You're not as bad as other people
- You're in control, as it's not every day
- You deserve some pleasures in life
- You don't need to listen to anyone's view on this
- You can think about this another time
- You can start next week, now isn't a good time
- You have failed before, you won't be able to do this.

Neither I, nor any other therapist in the land, will be able to dictate to you what constitutes a problematic habit. Only you can identify this.

When you're able to acknowledge a problem, you are on the road to recovery.

REMIND YOURSELF THAT YOU'RE ENOUGH

Underlying many habits is an innate sense of not being enough. Habits can be a means of running away from something, and often that something is you. Reminding yourself that you are enough can be a useful anchor for the times when you wobble. For example, if you repeatedly need to prove yourself or achieve successes to demonstrate your worth or value, maybe it is about coming back to the essential truth that you are 'enough'. By this I mean knowing that you matter and accepting yourself as you are is a crucial step to happiness. This will help you feel steady and prevent you from using your old habits to fill that void. When you regularly remind yourself that you are enough, in time you start to believe it. Remember, no matter how much you anaesthetize, avoid, hide or run away from yourself, eventually you have to come back there. I have run a few marathons in my life, literal marathons, and a few metaphorical ones where I've run away from myself. Coming back is really the only way.

CREATE HEALTHIER SURROUNDINGS

When making changes in life, it's never just about the decisions you make. When you're working on addressing your unhelpful habits, you'll also have to evaluate other aspects of life: the people you engage with, your environment, your schedule, how you plan. All of these factors, and others pertinent to you, will be important.

WEAN YOURSELF OFF YOUR HABIT

Whatever habit you're working on, whether it's drinking too much, working excessively or seeking power, the next stage is to start gradually reducing your reliance on, and the frequency with which you perform, some of your old habits. This won't be easy at first, which is why gradual reduction is important.

I want to add a specific comment here regarding reduction of substances such as alcohol, medication or drugs: please always seek professional guidance before starting this. Medical support may be needed in any programme of reduction to help manage 'cold turkey' (physical withdrawal) symptoms.

Back to more general guidance: once you've decided to work on a habit, I suggest that you set out a plan for weaning yourself off of it. This will enable you to work within a structure that is manageable for you and to track your progress. Often 'slow and steady' wins the race here. Many habits will have been ingrained for quite a long time. Gradual, phased reductions of old habits will help you establish new habits at a sensible pace. Many of the reports on dieting, for example, show that drastic quick-fix diets rarely work in the long term. For example, if you practise an unhelpful habit five times a day, then maybe reduce to four times daily for the first few days and so on. It might also be useful to join a support group, share your intentions with someone or start to keep a journal of progress.

LEARN TO SELF-SOOTHE

In its simplest form, self-soothing means going inward to find solutions to manage some of the difficult emotions or experiences in your life. For example, a client of mine, George, used gambling as a method to cope with his life, as he found it difficult to manage some painful emotions from his past. Gambling was his external means of soothing but in therapy we worked on how he could relate to his internal pain using healthier *self*-soothing methods. These included adapting his internal voice to be kinder to himself, using relaxation methods to quieten his mind, regulating his gambling, reserving judgement of himself and his circumstances, and processing some past experiences that triggered feelings of shame.

Self-soothing has different meanings for different people so use whatever methods work for you. Put simply it is self-actions, words, changes, habits or behaviours that help you feel more at ease. For one person it could be going to yoga, another a long walk or someone else meditation. As long as the act of self-soothing comes from a place of compassion, kindness and non-judgement, you won't go wrong. I can confidently say that when you learn to self-soothe and respond to yourself with some degree of compassion and kindness, everything changes.

Most people regularly treat themselves appallingly by continuously self-deprecating, self-judging or self-critiquing. In short, beating themselves up. This has to stop. When you are tough on yourself, you create a tough life. No one has ever experienced happiness following this path. I have a mantra that I try to follow: if I wouldn't say or do it to someone else, knowing it could hurt him or her, then I won't say or do it to myself.

ADOPT HEALTHIER HABITS

I mentioned earlier that not all habits are unhealthy. Replacing some habits with healthier alternatives is a great option. If it enhances body, mind and spirit in a way that works for you, without negative consequences, then go for it.

IDENTIFY THE SUPPORT YOU NEED TO KICK YOUR UNHEALTHY HABIT FOR GOOD

This will depend largely on what habits you're focussing on and the extent of the habit. However, all the key studies on addiction show that support systems such as therapy, groups, communities and dedicated programmes improve recovery. Even if you only share your intentions with one person, you're making the process a less solitary experience. It might be helpful to set up a system that allows you to share your progress with another person or group of people, or you could ask another person to check in with you regularly to incentivize you to stay on track. Try to select someone encouraging, non-judgemental and supportive. The last thing you need is someone giving you a hard time or judging you! None of us need that.

ALLOW FOR BAD DAYS

Unquestionably you will have days when things don't go to plan. Life will get in the way with changes or unexpected ups and downs. In a period of transition or change it is important to make allowances for wobbles. This will give you permission to get it wrong or simply have a bad day. More importantly, it will allow you to start again the next day, rather than catastrophize or 'throw in the towel'. Permanently changing long-term habits requires patience, understanding and flexibility. Some of the most successful people in history describe failing as part of their success. Success isn't about never making a mistake; it's about the ability to get back up. Don't be afraid to fall sometimes and assume bad days as a normal part of the process. Bad days can be sources of great wisdom!

HOW THIS WILL CONTRIBUTE TO YOUR HAPPINESS

I know from my work that unhelpful or unhealthy habits never solve the real issues that you're using them to distract you from or ease the symptoms of. When you stop, reduce or tweak habits (whatever is needed) you will become happier. Why? Because you are free from 'safety behaviours'. This term is often used in the world of anxiety management but it's equally relevant to happiness. The habits you are hooked on are safety behaviours and offer a quick fix or 'hit' that offers short-lived relief from your anxiety or unhappiness. But they're a metaphorical plaster on your issues, not a cure, and won't make you happy in the true sense or in the long term.

Without the anaesthetizing effects of your safety behaviours, you may initially feel deeply uncomfortable but you will also be experiencing your true, authentic self. When you don't avoid feeling your naturally occurring emotions, you are more present in your life. This is an essential aspect of true happiness. You are turning up for your life and experiencing it fully, as it is. Not only that but you will become stronger and more resilient as you discover you can successfully navigate the landscape of your life without crutches.

Happiness isn't just a state of mind; it's something you can contribute to with every choice you make. I think one of the most exciting aspects of our humanity is knowing that we have the power to opt in for this.

COMMITMENT

Vague intentions to make life changes rarely come to much. When dealing with changes in habits, dedication is necessary. If you think back to Chapter

2, when I discussed the brain, you will remember how hardwired we are. If you're serious about changing your unhelpful habits, you will need to start rewiring you brain to respond in different ways. Everything you do and every decision you make can help you achieve this. Essentially you are creating new hardwired systems. For example, if you're stressed and normally drink a bottle of wine in the evenings to cope, then your brain is hardwired to that response. When you reduce or stop (whatever you need to do), you immediately create a new response system, which will impact on how your neuropathways transmit information. Each time you opt for an alternative response, you will help solidify changes at a neurological level. This will help create new habits.

A commitment to healthier responses is non-negotiable and consistency is essential.

So, in whatever way is helpful for you, write down the intention you're committing to and what the healthier alternative might be. I suggest you read this commitment every day as a reminder or have it on you at all times so you can easily revisit it when you're struggling.

CASE STUDY

This case study relates to a group of young adult offenders I worked with. There were eight young men in the group, aged eighteen to twenty-two. They had two habits in common:

1. They all were involved in habitual crime.
2. They were all using drugs excessively.

I used a cognitive behavioural therapy (CBT) approach with the group and developed what is known as a group formulation. A formulation is a mapping out of a person's story and its purpose is to make sense of behaviours and what maintains them. Essentially CBT focuses on the effect our thoughts have on our emotions and behaviours.

Core themes emerged in the group that every participant identified with, which helped make sense of what was going on.

When it came to exploring what had happened in the past in the lives of each of the men, it transpired that all had experienced the following:

- Poverty
- Abandonment
- Instability at home
- A history of criminal activity dating back to early teenage years

Leading to feelings of:

- Abandonment issues
- Low self-worth and value
- Anger
- Anxiety about the future.

When it came to the role of unhelpful habits (crime and drug use), the following was identified:

- Both were viewed as a means of coping.
- Both stopped them dealing with feelings.
- Both provided some sense of identity.
- Crime helped them express their frustration.
- Both were viewed as a means of survival.
- Drugs provided a sense of soothing.
- Crime provided a sense of achievement.
- Both provided distraction.

Finally, when it came to exploring the potential consequences of crime and drugs, the entire group had experienced the following:

- Criminal records
- Unemployment
- Worsening sense of self-worth
- Symptoms of anxiety and depression when 'coming down' from drugs
- Emotional detachment (inability to identify feelings)

- Fragmented personal and family relationships
- General sense of unhappiness and dissatisfaction.

Of course, this group are a relatively extreme example when it comes to unhealthy habits but I hope this story illustrates the impact of the choices we make and demonstrates that their choices contributed to their unhappiness. With this in mind, I encourage you to seek to understand your habits with compassion, as, above all, this will help most.

As a group, we worked on all the key issues I outlined. After several weeks, the majority of the group began the process of reducing their drug intake via an organized programme and ceased their involvement in crime (as far as I was aware). After three months of treatment, six of the group showed significant improvements in their mood, their habits were under control, and they all started to re-evaluate their futures.

Two of the group dropped out after several weeks, which sadly can happen when people are unable to commit to change.

Above all, I hope this case study is a reminder that there is a story behind every behaviour; a choice with every habit; a way forward with every situation. Kicking the habits that are holding you back can truly kick-start your journey to a happier life!

SUMMARY

- It is important to identify and understand your unhelpful habits.
- Many of these habits are automated and used as coping strategies.
- Wean yourself off your habits gradually at a pace that is comfortable for you.
- Seek help when needed.
- Remind yourself that you are enough.
- Find alternative healthier habits.

- Self-soothe techniques will help.
- Remember the cost of unhealthy habits.
- You have control over how you manage your habits. You equally have control over how you contribute to your personal happiness with the choices you make.

CHAPTER 7

STOP BLAMING AND TAKE RESPONSIBILITY

I bet if I were to ask why you're occasionally unhappy, you would instantly be able to give me a list of reasons. I'm almost certain the list would include at least some the following:

- Other people's behaviour
- Difficult life events
- A superstitious sense of being 'unfortunate' (i.e. feeling that terrible things always happen to me)
- Losses (grief, relationships, friends, jobs)
- Financial burdens
- Stress

- Disappointments
- A sense of injustice and people treating me unfairly
- Background, family, culture, religion
- The challenges of the world at large, be they political, social or economic

Here's another interesting question for you. *How do you contribute to your own unhappiness?* I'm asking because it's highly likely you are a key contributor. The first time someone asked me that question, in my own therapy (I was in my early twenties), I was bloody furious! How dare they suggest that I would choose to be unhappy or even contribute to my own unhappiness! I'd had a tough time growing up and things weren't always easy. I was in for a surprise when I discovered that I was more instrumental in my unhappiness than I'd first realized.

If you feel a little angry with me at the moment, I get it. In my line of work, I've been called every name under the sun so if some of what I say makes you a little uncomfortable or angry, that's normal and healthy. Worthwhile change rarely feels fluffy at first.

Let's come back to the question. I'm asking you to trust me with this and see what comes to mind. For now, scribble a response to the question in your journal – just go with whatever comes to mind for you. We will look at the same question again later.

Would you believe me if I told you that this question was the most helpful one ever put to me in my own therapy? It was and here's why.

I learnt it was so much easier for me to place the blame for my unhappiness on my past struggles, negative experiences and rejections rather than on how I thought and behaved in the here and now. When I placed responsibility for my happiness on all the experiences outside of me, then I didn't have to take full responsibility. It was always someone or something else, not me. I was a victim, of sorts, in life and there was nothing I could do about this. Why shouldn't I be allowed to wallow in self-pity from time to time?

The answer is simple: because it was keeping me stuck and limiting me. I didn't have the emotional insight or knowledge to recognize this at the time. I have since discovered that my happiness is *my* responsibility. The more I blame, the more likely it is that everything will stay the same. The more I take responsibility, the more empowered I feel.

This is also true of almost every client who walks into my therapy office. I start off by asking, 'Why do you think you are struggling?' Apart from the occasional 'I'm paying you to tell me that' response, the norm is a long list of life events. I rarely hear a client start by taking any responsibility for his or her own actions or responses.

Each story is of course valid and all the life events or circumstances listed at the start of the chapter can justifiably *contribute* to a sense of personal unhappiness arising in the first place. But the *maintenance* of unhappiness, longer term, is often in the client's hands. This is also likely true of you.

I know this is hard to hear but you are the solution to moving through what's keeping you stuck. I could feed you a lot of 'pseudo-science' baloney, telling you it will all get better or to just leave it all to the universe and chant happy thoughts. That would be like trying to convince you Santa Claus exists!

I chatted to a woman at a party a few months back and made the cardinal mistake of telling her what I do for a living. It's one thing being a therapist, but add 'self-help author' and it's a whole new level of 'Can you fix my life?' Within ten minutes I'd heard her life story and that she was genuinely sad and dissatisfied with her life. She wanted a new career, a relationship and to move away from London. I knew she was suffering and I didn't want to be rude so I chatted with her for a while. I asked what she was doing to achieve her goals.

There was a silence, then she answered, 'Nothing.' She said she was just hoping that one day it would all happen. But it wasn't happening, and she wasn't taking any responsibility for making it happen. She had experienced a bad relationship a few years earlier and most of the blame for her current predicament was placed on that. She was stuck and the magical solution she was seeking was unlikely to come about.

The moment you accept that the *contributors to your unhappiness*, which caused it to arise, don't need to have a leading role in the *maintenance of your future unhappiness*, then you are free.

Please don't think I'm underestimating or minimizing in any way your suffering, pain, struggles, heartache or losses, or saying your feelings aren't totally justified. I know how painful and tough life can be. My message in this chapter is primarily about exploring with you how the darker times or experiences can be used to shape your life in the best possible way, rather than keep you powerless and in pain.

Recently I heard someone talk about Oprah Winfrey's early life, which included hardship, racism, abuse, loss and many great struggles. Fast-forward to today and she has created an inspirational life that isn't defined by adversity. Her life is based on learning, hope and salvaging all she can from the pain in her life.

I recently had a disagreement with a mental wellness support group organizer. They advocated that people with anxiety needed to be listened to and allowed to talk about concerns as often as was necessary. They also deemed suggestions such as yoga or mindfulness insulting to anxiety sufferers. The person was essentially suggesting that unhappy people should be allowed to immerse themselves in their suffering as much as they wanted, and be offered an abundance of empathy.

I entered a discussion about this, explaining that I agreed that listening and empathy are extremely important but that people with anxiety also need tips and techniques on how to help themselves. I went on to explain that encouraging a person to repeat their worries verbally multiple times can lead to those worries being reinforced and increase anxiety. It can also intensify reliance on safety-seeking behaviours (such as reassurance seeking), which worsens anxiety. The same applies for managing mood. All the evidence tells us that encouraging rumination and going over the same negative content again and again makes people unhappier.

Needless to say, the person wasn't happy with

my response. But I simply cannot agree with their suggestion that we ought to placate unhappy people, offer them infinite empathy and prevent them from moving forward. That's a sure-fire way of helping them stay stuck, dependent and powerless for the sake of appearing nice and empathetic. It's not doing the person suffering any favours, and it's not going to help longer term.

I want to help you understand that it is *you* who will need to do the work. If I collude with you in supporting endless blaming and not encouraging you to take some personal responsibility for your life, then I am not helping you.

There comes a point during a period of suffering when you have a choice: you can come out from under the warm, comfortable duvet of blaming and decide to start again, or you can stay where you are. My suggestions here aren't intended to be uncaring and I hope they don't read that way. I'm sharing with you what I know from experience works to help you reclaim a sense of control and direction in your life. You can't change any of what happened in your life but you can change how you manage it.

WHY WE BLAME OTHER PEOPLE AND CIRCUMSTANCES, AND STOP TAKING RESPONSIBILITY FOR OUR HAPPINESS

As you'll be familiar by now, I want to start by helping you understand *why* you might use a mechanism that's not working in your best interest, as is often the case with attributing blame.

Without doubt, blaming is, more often than not, an unconscious process. Put another way, it's something you might not even be aware that you're doing. It's an automatic response, and one that has cunning ways of convincing you it's right. The language of blaming places you in the role of victim, the aggrieved one or the person deserving of pity. As hard as it is to hear, this can be quite comfortably uncomfortable. I'll explain this as it's an odd concept to get your head around.

Sometimes in life, it can feel comfortable to be in a position in which the blame isn't yours and the automatic response from others is kindness, sympathy or empathy. To be fair, who wouldn't want this some of the time? It's almost your due compensation from life for delivering adverse events or circumstances. It also allows you to stay angry, which can sometimes feel like a righteous, powerful emotion. It comes, though, with a downside, in that it can leave you feeling disempowered and stuck if you continue to stay with this feeling longer term.

Placing blame upon people and events outside of yourself is used as a coping strategy or justification for one's behaviour for a variety of reasons (also known as blame motivators). It's possible you might have a few. From my clinical experience, the blame motivators I see most are:

- **Victim paralysis.** You become stuck in a belief that you have been victimized and that is the role you should play.
- **Identity attachment.** You may have developed an identity you're comfortable with that revolves around you having been wronged by other people and being the victim of bad luck. This happens for several reasons but one might be because that identity ensures you're treated with kindness and pity.
- **Avoidance.** You may engage with blame to justify disengagement from other aspects of your life. For example, 'I can't leave the house because something bad happened to me when I left the house a year ago.'

- **Powerfully powerless.** You might use blame as a means of holding power over situations or people. For example, people have to walk on eggshells around you and are made to feel guilty if they challenge what you say, do or believe, because of what happened to you.
- **Secondary gain.** You might discover that staying with blame has other benefits for you and allows you to steer situations to your advantage.

I'll expand on these a little more as it's important to understand how subtle the blame mechanism can be.

VICTIM PARALYSIS

Phil was a patient of mine who was bullied as a teenager because of his weight. As an adult, he developed a belief that everyone in life treated him unfairly and judged him based on his size. He described conflict in all areas of his life. Phil was often defensive without any real provocation because he felt people were treating him badly. Of course, this made him very unhappy and in therapy he uncovered that the key issues were his belief that he was a victim, alongside his misinterpretation of how everyone else saw him. This blame he placed on others kept him emotionally paralyzed.

IDENTITY ATTACHMENT

Blaming is frequently a long-standing pattern that becomes a dominant part of one's identity, and it occasionally results in other parts being lost. I had an acquaintance who was very badly injured in a terrorist bomb attack. She was understandably angry at first, but five years on, was still blaming the incident for ruining her life. At one point, her husband suggested she consider getting help to move on and get her life back. She was furious at this suggestion and couldn't understand why he would want her to move on from the terrible event that had occurred. Unconsciously, she had become attached to blaming the event for ruining her entire life and struggled to even consider moving forward.

AVOIDANCE

Blaming comes with a certain degree of power. If you have been wronged or hurt in some way, then it can earn you the right to opt out of the inconvenient or difficult parts of life that you would ordinarily want to opt out of anyway. I worked with a client, Jack, whose wife of forty years had died. Prior to her death, Jack described himself as generally angry and antisocial, something his family struggled with for many years. It was also something he never took any responsibility for. When his wife died, Jack blamed his loss for making him disengage more socially and sometimes behave in a rude, disrespectful way to his family. For the first year after his wife's death, the family understood but three years on, they became weary and relationships became frayed. During therapy, Jack discovered that he was attributing blame for his behaviours to his grief and loss. In truth, he was refusing to take any responsibility for behaviours that existed long before his bereavement.

POWERFULLY POWERLESS

I see this a lot in my clinical practice. When I am encouraging people to make changes or begin the process of letting go, there can be a power struggle, almost a tug of war! They might want to hold on to difficult events because in doing so, they can justify never putting themselves through the discomfort of change. It's not uncommon to hear 'But I can't because . . .' or 'I won't be able to because . . .' or 'You can't suggest I do this, because . . .'. I describe this as wishing to remain powerfully powerless as the client is attempting to hold on to the power of not changing, while remaining powerless as they are.

SECONDARY GAIN

I treated Sarah for post-traumatic stress disorder (PTSD) following a car accident. She was bedbound for one year and out of work for two years following the accident. Towards the end of therapy, she was fully recovered physically and her PTSD treated successfully. In our penultimate session together, Sarah's mood deteriorated and she started to relive old anger issues in relation to the driver of the car who crashed into her. It was a very extreme deterioration that didn't feel linked to her trauma. She became very angry, leading to an outburst blaming the driver for destroying her life, stating she couldn't go back to work and wanted to be back home in bed. After I explored this with Sarah, she truthfully acknowledged that she had enjoyed being away from work and enjoyed the love and care bestowed on her by her family while she was recovering. She didn't want it to end and was mourning some of the secondary gains.

I hope these case studies help you understand some of the subtle underlying processes that are occurring when you get caught up in patterns of blame and struggle to take ownership for moving forward. I know some of this is uncomfortable to take on board, but conscious awareness will move you closer to a happier state of being.

With that in mind, let's now look at how you go about dealing with blaming and taking responsibility for your happiness.

HOW TO STOP BLAMING AND TAKE RESPONSIBILITY

As always, I'll go through this using a step-by-step process, and you can use whatever works for you most effectively. I'll be using aspects of teachings from a model of therapy called acceptance and commitment therapy (ACT), which I feel is most useful in this area. The four areas we'll work through are:

- Acceptance
- What have you learnt?
- What personal values can you use to move you forward?
- Taking responsibility

ACCEPTANCE

I want to start by saying that when I talk about acceptance I'm not suggesting a passive or dismissive approach to any of the key events or difficulties you have experienced in life. I know you may have experienced some awful traumas, losses, bereavements, hardships, injustices and many other painful life events. These will have contributed to deep suffering and I can imagine the concept of just accepting might at first sound a little barbaric. I promise, wholeheartedly, this is not the case.

I worked with Chloe, who had lost a child. I can't even begin to imagine the depth of her pain. When we came to work on acceptance, she was furious, screaming that she would never accept the loss of her child. She blamed God, worried that she was a bad person and as she sobbed, falling to the floor, she suddenly, said, 'If I accept this has happened, I have to accept that my baby isn't coming back, and I never want to forget him.' That was the start of our work. That day Chloe realized that accepting the loss didn't mean she would ever forget her baby but she also realized that she had stopped living. My work with her focussed on accepting the awful reality of her loss. The acceptance not only helped her manage her pain but also gave her permission to start living again.

Every day of my career I hear refusals to accept life events or circumstances as they are, and these often go hand-in-hand with blame:

- If they hadn't done that, I would be fine.
- I will never forgive them. They destroyed me.
- I can't accept this loss and I blame God or whoever is out there!
- It's not my fault. It's all the things that are going on around me.
- I blame my parents. They screwed me up.
- I blame my past. I didn't choose that life.

The problem is, blaming doesn't resolve anything, even if it *is* warranted, because at some point acceptance is necessary. Whatever has happened in your life can't be changed. It can't be undone. Acceptance doesn't mean that it should have happened or that it's right or fair. It means you are willing to come to terms with life as it is.

There is an expression in many twelve-step programmes: 'Help me to accept the things I cannot change.' I believe there is great wisdom in that.

You may have something in your life that you've spent a lot of time blaming others and bad luck for, and as a result, you haven't been able to take responsibility for moving forward. Maybe now is the time to consider accepting the reality of what is.

This is your life and perhaps you owe it to yourself to allow yourself permission to live it.

WHAT HAVE YOU LEARNT?

If the blame game is resonating with you, I imagine you might be quite familiar with the emotions that tend to come with it: anger, resentment and resistance. These of course will work to make your position – the blame you're apportioning – seem even more justified. How about taking a different stance and considering what you've learnt from all the adversities that you've got stuck in a pattern of blame with? Immediately you move from a position of powerlessness and blame to power-reclaiming.

A useful way of considering this is to list what you have learnt and then translate that into everyday life. Areas worth considering are:

> - Coping strategies that helped.
> - What support systems helped you?
> - How did you manage each day?
> - Who were the people in your life that helped you?
> - What types of thinking made things more manageable?
> - What self-resources helped you?

When I do this work with clients they often (re)discover character traits they didn't know they had:

- Resilience
- Strength
- Hope
- Courage
- Adaptability
- Ability to forgive

Maybe now is the time to stop asking 'How have I been wronged?' Today you can ask, 'What have I learnt?'

WHAT PERSONAL VALUES CAN HELP MOVE YOU FORWARD?

We all have values that fit in with our purpose, reason for living and contribution to life at large. My values will be different from yours so there's no one-size-fits-all solution to offer here. Have you ever, though, stopped and wondered what makes you tick in life? What matters to you? What's important? What type of person you want to be remembered as?

I facilitated on a self-development programme last year and one of the group, Simon, shared a powerful story that has stayed with me. He talked openly about living a very miserable existence for the larger part of his life, attributing it to a very turbulent, impoverished childhood. He described feeling as if life had dealt him a 'raw deal', leading to a defeatist perspective fuelled by a lot of blaming and feeling victimized.

One day at home, his eleven-year-old son was doing homework for a school project on the local graveyard. His son suddenly asked Simon what he would like the epitaph on his gravestone to read. Simon didn't know how to answer at first but without thinking he suddenly spluttered out, 'He made a difference.' He noted his son smirked, and in that moment, he realized that he wasn't living the values for the life he wanted. His patterns of blaming, self-pity and anger didn't serve a purpose for his life. He was forced to re-evaluate and start taking responsibility, which made an enormous difference to his life.

What would you want your epitaph to read? Do you think you live your life according to your current values? If not, you have an opportunity to do something about it.

TAKING RESPONSIBILITY

As a therapist, there is a crossroads moment with most clients when I realize they might run for the hills or stay with the work. That moment normally occurs when it dawns on them that I won't 'fix' them. It's a big moment but a necessary one. I've had a few runaway clients in my time. Most return a few weeks later.

I think the same likely happens when reading a book like this, particularly with the work we are doing in this chapter. This is your opportunity to recognize that blaming and failing to take responsibility are creating obstacles to your happiness – if indeed that is what's happening. If they are, then you've taken a huge step by simply acknowledging this fact. If this chapter has offered you some valuable insights, then you have a choice to do something different. You have the option to continue as you are or start again. You have the option to be happier.

HOW THIS WILL CONTRIBUTE TO YOUR HAPPINESS

To write this section I decided to reflect on every case I've worked on in which blaming and lack of responsibility were dominant factors. What surprised me was how regularly I see this! The good news is that most people's state of mind improves dramatically once they experience how beneficial letting go of blame is. Here is how it will contribute to your happiness:

- Blame is a negative emotion allied with anger. When it lessens, you will experience a sense of ease and peace.
- Blame is associated with powerlessness. When you begin to let it go you will feel empowered.

- Blame will keep you stuck. Letting go will help you experience a new sense of freedom.
- A refusal to take responsibility for your life limits you. When you start taking responsibility, new possibilities emerge.
- Not taking responsibility means that you hand over control of your life to other people and external factors. When you take responsibility, you gain a greater sense of control and say in your life.
- Not taking responsibility always weakens your position. Taking responsibility will make you feel stronger and empowered.

COMMITMENT

I don't want to labour the point of taking responsibility, which I hope is clear at this stage. Your commitment to this is, of course, essential. The only reminder I do want to add is that many of your old patterns will likely be quite firmly ingrained, so unlearning takes regular, daily commitment. Stay mindful of falling back into old patterns. They will feel comfortable and familiar but that doesn't mean they are helpful. Blaming and not taking responsibility is such an easy trap to fall into. Stay vigilant of this.

It might be useful to keep a journal every day, write a blog, record yourself talking or use whatever medium works best for you. The point is to keep track of your progress and have something daily that is a reminder of your commitment.

CASE STUDY

I struggled when deciding what story to share with you for this chapter as I've so many to choose from. Then it dawned on me that the most powerful example I have isn't so much an example as an analogy: my experience of growing up in Northern Ireland. For context, my formative years (1969–1990) coincided with The Troubles. There was serious violence and conflict between Protestants and Catholics over a long-standing disagreement (the disagreement, although not the violence, is still ongoing). During the period of conflict 3,000 people died, many of them innocent civilians. The central disagreement is that Protestants believe Northern Ireland should be governed by the UK because they identify as British. Catholics, on the other hand, identify as Irish, so they believe the Irish government should govern all of Ireland, including Northern Ireland.

I think it's important to say that the majority of people, regardless of what they believed, had no interest in perpetuating the violence and conflict. Politicians and terrorist groups, however, fuelled the division with an endless onslaught of blaming, with neither side taking any real responsibility for peace. An IRA ceasefire ended this in 1994, followed by the Good Friday Agreement in 1998 when both sides agreed to talk, compromise, understand each other more, and stop with the blame game.

My entire childhood and adolescence was saturated in a political culture of blame and reckless, irresponsible behaviour. The outcome for everyday people was:

- Loss
- Trauma
- Division
- Fear
- Unhappiness
- Anger
- Inability to live fully.

The Northern Ireland conflict was very real but it is also an analogy for a life lived in a constant state of blaming others, and not taking responsibility for actions and choices.

If this chapter has helped you identify that you are at war with yourself (and not, in fact, other people or the world), then maybe it's time for your personal ceasefire. When the blaming stops, and you take ownership over your life, it can open the way to peace and a greater sense of happiness. You can form your own **Good Friday Agreement** with yourself and can create a better tomorrow.

SUMMARY

- There are underlying reasons why you are blaming other people and circumstances, and not taking responsibility for your life and happiness.
- Blaming does not bring about positive outcomes.
- Four steps for managing this are: acceptance, reflecting on what you have learnt, using values to move you out of this pattern and taking responsibility.
- Letting go of blaming will improve your life and make you happier.

CHAPTER 8

COMPARISON IS THE THIEF OF JOY

Most of us have periods when we feel very happy with life but we can easily fall into the trap of comparing our lives to other people's. This can contribute to feeling unhappy, telling ourselves that we'll be happier at some point in the future if we have more of what other people have. When this happens, happiness is compromised because we are living in a state of 'lack'. What I mean by that is that we become focussed on what we don't have, rather than on what we do.

When we compare our life to others', we always discover we are lacking something. Inevitably, there will always be other people who appear be having a better time or are more successful. So, we tell ourselves that what we have now isn't enough and then seek more.

I decided to write this chapter after I witnessed a group of six mums and their toddlers chatting in my local coffee shop. I was sitting, writing this book, when they positioned themselves at the table next to me. I learnt a lot about the children in a very short space of time. According to the parents, Jacob had learnt many more words than other children his age, Rosie was very bright for her age and Tommy had started walking much sooner than his peers. Yes, the comparisons had started as the mums battled it out to determine who had the 'superchild.'

Seeking more was also on the agenda as the mums debated the best schools, the best child care options and all the extra-curricular activities available in the local area. It seemed all of the children were borderline genius at most activities. Who knew two-year-old Tommy could be identified as a budding rugby star at Rugger Kidz? Who knew Rosie had the potential to be the next Judy Garland according to Star Makers?

I learnt a lot that day as I sipped my latte, eavesdropping intently on the conversations. All of these children were going to learn to compare, compete and seek more from life. Whilst that's fine if balanced out by an awareness of what you *do* have, if not, it can make you very unhappy.

I'm not a parent and I can't judge these parents who all clearly wanted the best for their children. But the things I didn't hear discussed were fun, freedom, choice or enjoying being in the moment of parenting these kids. Everyone had something to prove and every child was going to be super-special, whether they liked it or not!

I don't think we can be happy unless we feel at ease and are satisfied with what we have.

Sure, we'll feel bursts of happiness at major life events like our wedding day, the birth of our children, when we take part in those super-fun activities like going on holiday or having a spontaneous wild night out with old friends but these activities are few and far between, particularly as you get older and have more responsibilities and commitments. Most of the time we're going about life as normal and if you're relying on the super-fun things to give you your happiness quota, you're going to be disappointed. If, on the other hand, you've created a life where you experience a sense of deep contentment as you go about your day-to-day, this ultimately translates into happiness, even joy.

For me, contentment can be found sitting stroking my dog, walking along the river with my partner, having a night at home by the fire or drinking a cup of tea in my local deli! I've noticed that the simpler I keep things, the easier it is to be happier.

Now might be a good time to ask yourself whether comparing or wanting more gets in the way of your happiness. Perhaps you find yourself regularly being plagued by one or more of these thoughts:

- I am not as happy as others.
- I should have achieved more in my life by now.
- I am having less fun and excitement than others.
- I don't have enough money.
- I don't have a big enough house or flat.
- I don't have a life like those lucky people on television.
- I can't share my 'real' life on social media or publicly as it will appear 'crap' compared to everyone else.
- I don't have a body or the looks like the people in magazines.

- I don't have an exciting job like some people do.
- I don't have the perfect family, kids, partner.

If you're not comparing yourself to other people, then that voice in your head might be telling you that you will be happier in the future only:

- When you are living somewhere better.
- When you are earning more.
- When you have the perfect relationship.
- When you are more successful or famous, or once you receive recognition.
- When you are in a better place emotionally.
- When you have achieved the targets you've set yourself.
- When you get the bigger car.
- When you live in the dream house.
- When you are emotionally stronger.

The list of things we want more, or better versions, of is endless. To be fair, I do appreciate that some of the examples mentioned might help you feel happier. For example, if you are living in sub-standard living conditions and want a better home, a desire to improve your situation is, of course, reasonable. My point stands only when we fixate on bigger and 'better' situations in life when we already have adequate means for our happiness. Once you enter that place, it often becomes clear that each milestone reached is never enough.

Let me pause here to say that I'm not criticizing ambition or a desire for a better life, which can be a positive force. But do be aware if and when this desire for betterment tips over into becoming relentless and insatiable. That's when you know that 'wanting more' has become a means of masking underlying dissatisfaction.

I hate to burst your bubble but I'm going to. You *cannot* feel happy if you go through life comparing yourself to others or telling yourself you will be happier when certain conditions are fulfilled in the future. It doesn't work that way. Life doesn't offer those guarantees. Learning how to manage this will be a focus in this chapter.

The truth is that you, I and many others are part of 'generation discontent', living in a deluded state of believing that everyone else is happier, and something else will make our lives better. The reality is no one's life is perfect. If you believe it is, you are comparing yourself to an illusion that you don't know much about. Equally, nothing you pursue or desire will bring you happiness until you are at ease with yourself and able to let go of the underlying cause of your dissatisfaction.

If you're reading this book, you will likely be privileged enough to live in a developed country with access to money, health care, sanitation and a relatively high standard of living. I mention this not to shame anyone but as a reminder that we usually have enough to meet basic needs, something that often gets overlooked. If you struggle to appreciate the basic stuff, then everything beyond is going to be a struggle too.

It's not surprising that many headlines and research papers tell us that we in the so-called developed world are increasingly feeling overwhelmed, unhappy and dissatisfied and struggling to cope with life. But what's this all about? As a society, we have never been more advanced, sophisticated and wealthy, yet our emotional and psychological struggles appear greater. It would seem that the more we have, the more our happiness is compromised.

Do you ever wonder whether you leave enough space to experience joy as life increasingly becomes filled with more comparisons, noise, distractions, achievements, purchases and interactions? None of which, incidentally, ever seems to be enough!

As I'm writing this chapter, it's a few weeks to Christmas and I noticed in the shops today a frenzy of people wanting, seeking and desiring more of everything. At one point, I had the woman from the perfume counter spraying me like an assassin with a fragrance promising (and I quote) 'the smell of success for the modern man'. Who knew? All those years of hard work, when all that time success – or at least, the scent of it, whatever that is – was available in a bottle for the bargain price of £50! She also tried selling me another perfume 'for the lovely lady' in my life, not knowing, of course, the lovely lady in my life is a dog called Kate!

I treated a high-profile actor once. I'll call him Matthew. He'd had phenomenal success in his career, securing leading roles and receiving critically acclaimed reviews, and materially he had everything you could dream of. When we met, he was experiencing some anxiety and low mood symptoms. His goal in therapy was to feel a little happier. After several weeks, it became clear there were two key issues with him:

1. He was comparing his success to others whom he deemed more successful. It was making him desperately unhappy.

2. He was fearful his fame would end so he set out to achieve as much as he could whilst he was flourishing. Nothing was enough.

Here was someone, theoretically (according to the magazines), successful and happy. In reality, he was unhappy and lonely. His constant comparing and pushing for more was getting in the way of his life, impacting his mood and causing him anxiety. It was making him unhappy.

Matthew told me a story of attending an awards ceremony in which he had won best actor, and the announcement was greeted with a standing ovation. However, on the same evening, he was runner-up in a different category. He finished the evening alone in his apartment, drinking vodka, because he began comparing himself to the winning actor from the other category. His moment of happiness was sabotaged.

We worked together and over time he learnt to break these unhealthy patterns and started to experience true happiness whether he won an award or not.

The aim of this chapter is to wake you up to the consequences of endless comparison and wanting more, as you too may be unaware that you are sabotaging your own opportunities for happiness.

WHY DO WE COMPARE AND SEEK MORE?

Underlying psychological states fuel most unhealthy decisions, actions and thought processes. There are four states in particular that tend to be the trigger for comparing your life to others' or endlessly seeking more. They are:

1. Dissatisfaction
2. Desire
3. Self-doubt
4. Self-sabotage

I'll go into more detail about those in a moment but first a little detour to explore why we stay anchored in those states in the first place.

In short, modern advances, especially in the worlds of social media, TV and advertising, constantly remind us of what we don't have and what we apparently need. We are bombarded daily with images telling us what the 'norm' is and how we ought to look, behave, think and exist. Sadly the 'norms' portrayed are actually quite extreme and veer towards unrealistic perfection. This is something we can logically be aware of but it doesn't stop us wanting them.

I can look at David Beckham's social media account, buy his aftershave and wish for his life but does it move my own life forward? Of course it doesn't. It can, on the other hand, make me feel miserable if I compare my bank account, my body and my lifestyle to his, because we're told to believe, through the subliminal or explicit messaging in the text, image and video content, that this is achievable for everyone! This is a lie; it's not. Only a minuscule proportion of people can achieve this level of success, and it often isn't through lack of talent or even hard work that most don't make it. Worse still, we are persuaded that the bank account, the body and the lifestyle equal happiness.

And while these relatively new developments in how we receive information may not be the root cause of your feelings of dissatisfaction or self-doubt, they can certainly work to exacerbate negative feelings and keep them front of mind.

DISSATISFACTION

Think of a time when you have been feeling dissatisfied with your life. It could be as a result of feeling bored, unfulfilled or unappreciated. None of these feelings are nice so your natural instinct may be to escape.

This is when the comparison comes in. You might decide to browse a glossy magazine or scroll social media in this state of dissatisfaction. What starts as curiosity quickly becomes comparison to your own situation. You may justify this as seeking inspiration or having a nosey but ultimately you will compare your life to those you have peered into. The end result is even greater dissatisfaction and further blocks to your happiness.

When seeking more, your dissatisfaction could lead you, for example, to excessively spend money on items you want. You will of course convince yourself that spending money on these items is the answer to your dissatisfaction. Longer term, you will realize it hasn't worked, leaving you more dissatisfied.

DESIRE

Desire is a normal emotion, and it's healthy so long as it's not out of your control. Whatever it is you desire, it can feel like a ravenous hunger and the human drive is to satisfy that. The problem is, we are all now programmed to desire more of everything. Tech hardware, apps, games and social media platforms have been designed to make us addicted to the 'hit' we get off of interacting with them to the extent that we require constant stimulation — i.e. a desire-fulfilment loop — to stop us feeling bored, anxious and uncomfortable. We are rarely satisfied and always hungry for something.

It is therefore natural to desire what others have or seem to have. Subconsciously you will be in primal mode trying to work out how others are having their needs met. You will be instinctively driven to curiously compare your lot with theirs and may feel let down when your desires are not being met in the same way. This thought process might sound something like, Why isn't my life as good as his/hers? The times when you might feel envious of someone could actually mean you are hungry with desires that you see as unmet.

How desire leads to never being satisfied and perpetually seeking more is more obvious, and it arises from simply wanting more of everything that drives you. For some it can be sex, for some food, for others money or status. It is that excessive hunger for something that provides pleasure.

This mechanism can be very powerful if not managed with a degree of balance.

SELF-DOUBT

This is not new territory in this book but understanding how it links to comparing and seeking more is important.

When you doubt yourself in any way (which normally comes with giving yourself a tough time), you will seek out evidence to prove that your doubts are warranted. For example, if you're telling yourself that you aren't good enough or can't do something, then an easy way to gather evidence for that claim could be to compare yourself with others who are succeeding. This can, in a warped way, reinforce your belief that you're not enough in the first place. Essentially, comparing can be used to support your self-doubt and make you unhappier. How's that for a self-inflicted punch in the gut! It's incredible the tricks unhealthy patterns play on us!

It makes sense then, if you are filled with self-doubt, for you to excessively seek more in other areas of your life to help you distract or compensate for this feeling. In the world of psychology we call this compensatory avoidance and it's something most of us are very skilled at!

SELF-SABOTAGE

It might sound extreme to describe comparing yourself to others or seeking more as an act of self-sabotage but trust me, it can be.

Comparing ourselves to others is a powerful way of reinforcing self-loathing or self-criticism. The story in your head will encourage you to compare your own achievements, qualities and situation to others' successes, their beauty, their status or in fact anything you perceive yourself to be lacking in. It's well documented that many people report a lower mood state after browsing social media, even for a short period of time.

It's the same scenario with seeking more. You actively move towards a point where the amount of whatever it is you're seeking – whether it be food, sex, drugs, money or validation – becomes destructive, as an act of self-sabotage.

HOW TO STOP COMPARING AND SEEKING MORE

This may sound unusual but if reading this chapter is making you a little uncomfortable, I'm pleased. It means I'm doing my job. A client of mine once asked me if there was a version of therapy that isn't challenging. I told her there was and it was called 'fairy dust therapy', and would likely start producing results in the year 'twenty never'.

So let's stay away from glitter, fairy dust and sparkly happiness and work through how we can pull back from comparing and seeking more. This involves practising four very important steps daily:

- Gratitude
- Acts of kindness
- The art of simplicity
- Turning inwards for satisfaction

GRATITUDE

Without getting too bogged down in science, we know from the worlds of psychology and neuroscience that when we are grateful for what we have, we are happier. I could try to dress this up with fancy terminology but it's no more complicated than that. Scientifically we know gratitude wakes up a part of the brain called the hypothalamus and this improves grey matter on the righthand side of the brain. People with increased grey matter are likely to practise gratitude more, and people who practise gratitude have increased levels of serotonin and dopamine (feel-good chemicals). In short it's an interconnected process with positive benefits. This contributes to an overall state of wellness but also helps you gain a sense of perspective.

Gratitude, I promise, will make you feel happier but it's something that's often forgotten as our default setting is to look for the negative. Maybe the next time you find yourself comparing your life to others' and seeking more, stop and remind yourself what you can be grateful for in your life. In fact, stop now and ask yourself, 'What am I grateful for?' Make a note of what comes up in your journal. I suggest you start each day with that question.

You are not only changing your life, you are changing how your brain functions in a way that will be more helpful for you. This is the opposite of comparing yourself negatively to others and endlessly seeking more.

Today I woke up tired and a little grumpy but

when I practised gratitude I was reminded that I had a comfortable home, a great partner and dog, and running hot water! My mood shifted instantly and any desire to compare or seek more diminished. I have enough.

ACTS OF KINDNESS

Acts of kindness are a conscious decision to do something kind for another being without any secondary gain in return. In other words, there is nothing in it for you consciously . . . but, hang on a sec, maybe there is!

The science of acts of kindness is similar to gratitude in that you activate the same parts of the brain, resulting in a similar release of feel-good chemicals.

The act of doing something kind for another being removes you from your own need to compare or seek more, which has an automatic positive impact. It is also helpful to another person, which can add to a sense of satisfaction.

I witnessed this in a very powerful way many years ago. I was working with a group of young people who were very troubled, and let's just say that they were getting into quite a lot of mischief. An opportunity emerged for them to volunteer at a local homeless shelter, and the changes I witnessed in their behaviour after a few weeks were astounding. Volunteering removed them from their own sense of inadequacy and anger, changing both their perspective on themselves and their lives.

Perhaps today can be the day you start to practise a daily act of kindness in whatever way works for you. If you see something that moves you or upsets you, reach out and offer support. It could be a cup of tea for a workmate having a tough day, a smile to someone who looks lonely or a donation that helps a charity. It can be anything. But it's a world away from comparing, focussing on what you don't have and always wanting more.

Imagine how different our world would be if every person made this conscious decision as part of their day!

THE ART OF SIMPLICITY

I once had a fascinating conversation with a priest in his nineties a few weeks before he died. He told me he had one suitcase that was sufficient for all his possessions. He believed that was one of the main reasons he lived a happy life. When I asked him why, he said, 'Because our lives have become too cluttered. The less I carry, the less I'm burdened.'

I have never forgotten these words as they reveal why we become distressed when we seek to accumulate more and more stuff in the hopes of matching up to those we compare ourselves to. The more clutter in your life, the more you fear its loss.

I believe simplicity in life is an essential ingredient for happiness because it will help anchor you. When you are satisfied with simpler pleasures, you won't want to continue gathering more and more possessions.

I wonder how it might look for you to keep things a little simpler? I also wonder if your life has become bloated with too much of everything and little space to breathe or notice what you have?

In the spirit of truthfulness, there was a time when comparing myself to others and wanting more took me far away from the simplicity I talk of here. But nowadays I envy (in a positive way) those who have mastered the art of simple living because they are always happier people. The simpler I keep my life, the happier I am. This is something I now work on every day and it's prioritized way above achievements, successes or material gains.

Most of us compare ourselves to those who have more complex, crowded, successful lives; rarely do we compare ourselves to those living simpler lives. Maybe it's time to embrace simplicity a little more and discover the incredible wisdom to be found there.

TURNING INWARDS FOR SATISFACTION

The famous psychiatrist Jung once said that when we look outwards we dream, but when we go inwards we awaken. Wise words.

If you were satisfied with your internal world then you wouldn't be comparing your life to others' or on the prowl for more of whatever stimulates you. With that in mind, the solution seems clear.

When you find your satisfaction, peace, happiness or whatever you want to call it inside yourself, then you aren't reliant on external forces to make you happy. In some ways, you become master of your own destiny as everything you need is already within you; it's just having the courage to change direction and allow yourself to turn inwards.

That might sound a little scary, as going inwards may be unknown territory for you, but that's where you're most likely to find what you're looking for. And once you've found it, you won't feel the need to look for solutions outside yourself that the external world can't provide.

I appreciate that 'going inwards' may not make

a lot of sense or may sound a bit vague so I'm going to translate this into an everyday example.

Imagine a day when you are feeling low and a little lost. Your automatic default may be to distract yourself and start exploring what others are doing with their lives. Likewise, you might look for a way to numb some of the feelings with a few beers. But it doesn't bring you any answers.

Turning inwards on a day like this would see you stop, take time out, slowly breathe and lean into the feelings with curiosity to see what is there. It could involve asking yourself what you need. Within that, you might discover that the emotions are encouraging you to create space to process or deal with something. They might also be encouraging you to evaluate your self-care or waking you up to the direction you need to go, or any changes you might need to make. Can you see the difference? Turning inwards has the amazing potential to lead you to a place of clarity. It is learning to listen more to the voice within. This is another way for you tap into your potential for greater happiness.

HOW THIS WILL CONTRIBUTE TO YOUR HAPPINESS

The benefits to your life are myriad:

- Increased sense of wellbeing
- Positive changes in structure and functioning of your brain
- Renewed perspective
- Healthier use of time
- More space and openness in your life which influences your happiness
- Increased self-awareness
- Stops you seeking happiness from places you won't find it

COMMITMENT

Without doubt, there needs to be a daily commitment to the work in this chapter. This is a major lifestyle change and, as before, the consistency is what will ultimately change not only your mindset and behaviours, but also the actual functioning of your brain.

You might like to make a note in your journal or set a reminder on your phone to remember:

- **Gratitude.** Thinking of three things I'm grateful for today.
- **Acts of kindness.** Carrying out a good deed.
- **The art of simplicity.** Enjoying simple pleasures.
- **Turning inwards.** Noticing the emotions I'm experiencing today and what they're telling me.

Only you can do this work and I would earnestly encourage you to commit to the above. You will notice immeasurable positive changes in your life.

CASE STUDY

This isn't a client story as such, but a memory of an event back in 1985 when Bob Geldof organised Live Aid in response to the famine in Ethiopia. The event was broadcast to an estimated 1.9 billion people across 150 nations, watched by 40 per cent of the world's population. It had a positive humanitarian influence on foreign policy and challenged approaches to world hunger.

I was a teenager at the time of the event and watched in awe as the world came together to support people in need. At that moment, the only comparing going on was to those less fortunate and people were seeking to help others, not themselves.

I think the event was a lesson in selflessness but it also had aspects of everything I have talked about in this chapter: gratitude, kindness, simplicity and turning inwards.

Live Aid made us more grateful for what we had. It encouraged us to be kind. It forced us to be grateful for the simple things in our own lives as we watched people starve to death. But it challenged us to look inwards and explore our values and what mattered most.

This event reminded me how privileged my life was, even though my circumstances were less than ideal at that time. It was the ultimate lesson in perspective.

If you lose perspective, believing the grass is always greener, you will suffer endlessly.

Maybe some gratitude, kindness and a new perspective will bring you a few steps closer to suffering less, and living more. It may ease the pain that the constant comparing and wanting brings to you, me, all of us.

SUMMARY

- Comparing your life and situation to others' and constantly seeking more has a negative impact on your wellbeing.
- There are always underlying psychological processes that explain why you do this.
- Practising gratitude will have a positive impact on your state of mind.
- Acts of kindness will change your perspective.
- Simplicity will help declutter your life.
- Turning inwards will help you achieve more insight.

CHAPTER 9

HIGH-DRAMA LIVING

Shakespeare described the world as a stage and the people merely players. Day after day, we experience dramas, playing our parts. Some days we may be centre stage; other days, in the wings. Let's be honest about this, centre stage roles receive most of the adulation and applause, and this can be very desirable.

This is also true of real life. Drama can serve a purpose and become an addictive way of living as it often serves up intensity, passion and an escape from the monotony of everyday life. It shines a limelight of sorts that may not otherwise be there. Seeking out or creating drama is often an unconscious move – something you may not even be aware that you're doing. The problem is that it comes with a price as it impacts negatively on your happiness.

High-drama living is stressful living and often not conducive to a happy, peaceful lifestyle.

So far, I've discussed letting go of the following barriers to happiness:

- The past
- Unhelpful thinking
- Regrets
- Worry
- The negative influence of other people
- Unhelpful habits
- Blaming
- Comparing

In the course of our work on letting go of drama, we'll be touching upon all the areas we've covered so far. If the issue of drama isn't addressed, it's easy to fall back into old patterns within any one of the other areas that act as barriers to happiness. Essentially, addiction to drama is like the fuel that keeps many other problems going, so it can't be ignored.

In the world of acting, thespians tell us that drama

is conflict. I know a few television producers and they tell me that high drama makes the best television. We love to see conflict, tension, affairs, deception and all sorts of cliff-hangers. None of the characters in soap operas lead quiet 'normal' lives. It's all action-packed drama, which proves popular with viewers. However, it's worth noting that happiness is often in short supply, whereas dysfunction is plentiful.

I mentioned earlier I am writing this last section of the book as Christmas approaches. If the year was split up into fictional events it most represents, I would view Christmas, and the run up to it, as the drama Oscars. Every year I return to Ireland pre-Christmas to visit family and friends. The pantomime starts early. It's high drama at its best.

It's a very intense period as I observe various family and friends shop until midnight with frenzy in their eyes. I mean, this is serious business. If the supermarket runs out of goose fat to cook the turkey, Christmas is ruined. Worse still, I've witnessed complete meltdowns when Elsa, the doll from *Frozen*, isn't in stock! Not to mention fitting in work, Christmas carols, baking the cake and making sure every neighbour within a three-mile radius gets a card (even the ones that haven't been seen in ten years or may even have died)!

I haven't got to family dynamics yet. Who is hosting Christmas? Who hasn't replied to the Christmas drinks invite? Who has fallen out this year? Who can't be invited to the same event to avoid arguments?

All this drama for one day! It will, of course, end in exhaustion, stress, conflict, tears and the age-old pledge: 'Never again!'. That is, until next year.

In the meantime there is Valentine's Day, Easter, a wedding, a funeral and a summer holiday to plan. Events provide easy access to drama alongside all the everyday scenarios that also play a vital part.

I find addiction to drama really interesting because I've never met anyone who initially recognizes it as a problem for them. It's always life, people, events or circumstances, so this is an area I sometimes have to address. Woe betide anyone who tries to suggest differently. I raise the points no one wants to hear!

I met someone recently at a drinks event who shared with me how stressed and overwhelmed he was (and I believed him). Interestingly he told me about his twelve-hour workday, a 5 a.m. start for the gym, the pressure of paying for four holidays each year and private school fees for his children. Early into the conversation I recognized that despite the stress these parts of his life were causing, the guy had a boastful tone about his busyness and the demands of his lifestyle. His way of life was creating a dramatic intensity in his life, and he was over-identifying with this. He described stressful feelings and the negative impact on his life but the tone of his voice didn't fit with his description. I was curious about him.

In a well-intentioned manner, I decided to offer a suggestion. I acknowledged how stressful his life was and asked whether he'd considered shorter workdays, reducing the number of holidays he had and reviewing the private school options. I thought these were sensible suggestions. He didn't share my view. He immediately responded defensively, reminding me how busy he was, how mentally strong he was (despite his stress) and that he didn't need suggestions. He also told me few people understood 'high fliers' and that he was very happy with his life regardless. This time I didn't believe him.

He wasn't interested in solutions and my instinct was correct. He was addicted to the drama of his busy life but was unable to see the impact. My words certainly hit a raw nerve but he wasn't ready to hear them.

It's important to mention here, I may also hit a nerve with you. It's really uncomfortable to acknowledge when you may be hooked on drama.

I know this both personally and professionally. Some professionals often neglect this area because it is uncomfortable and can be deemed confrontational.

I'm not here to judge or scoff. I'm here to help you get unstuck from anything that interferes with your happiness. High-intensity drama does. If you aren't aware of this, then you can't do anything about it.

If you are currently wondering whether you are addicted to drama in your life, this is a healthy place to be. Curiosity can be a positive first step.

There isn't an exhaustive list of drama traits. Of course many link to other legitimate issues but my interest is in how drama can be a maintenance factor. In the span of my career I do see regular presentations that are habitual and can be changed. Some might resonate with you and some won't. The important point is to stop and consider whether engaging in any of the following impinges on your happiness and wellbeing:

- Repeatedly choosing the 'wrong' relationships despite advice and support from others.
- Excessive busyness that always leaves you overwhelmed and gets shared with everyone.

- Conflict with others – often due to misinterpretation or arguing for the sake of arguing.
- Fixation on how 'unlucky' you are and a tendency to share this with others.
- More interest in high-intensity events, e.g. emergency visits to see relatives in hospital but not when they are home. Similarly, attending funerals for people you barely know or haven't seen in a long time.
- Holding on to difficult or sad life events and repeatedly sharing with others.
- Exaggerating the impact of events on you (some you may have little involvement with).
- Over-sharing of 'big stories' on social media forums to attract interest, likes or comments.
- Use of extreme language that often includes words like awful, terrible, worst, bad, disaster, catastrophe.
- Getting involved in situations you know historically will lead to conflict or difficulties.
- Refusing support or dismissing helpful suggestions.

- Relishing your own misfortune or that of others.
- Excessive gossip about others that can lead to conflict or division.

I know some of these are tough to digest and might activate some very uncomfortable reactions. If they do, stop and listen to the emotional response they're generating. There may be something hugely important here that'll help you break down the blocks to your happiness. Don't rush through this section. Instead note down the statements that have made you most uneasy. This will be helpful to come back to. Some will overlap with work in previous chapters but my interest now is whether holding on to drama is keeping you stuck or being used in an unhealthy way. Make a note in your journal.

Like everything we have worked on so far, there are underlying psychological reasons why you might engage in some of these statements and understanding this is an important part of letting go. I'm going to break them down into common themes.

WHY YOU HOLD ON TO DRAMA

This is not an exhaustive list but my experience is that there are five dominant psychological processes at play that can help explain behaviours that are consistent with excessive drama. As always there will be short-term gains and long-term consequences. The five processes are:

1. Avoidance
2. Compensatory mechanisms
3. Attention-seeking
4. Constructed identity
5. Hereditary patterns

The processes will play out in different ways for different people – with accompanying varying behaviours – but as you read through them, notice your reactions. With anything that resonates strongly with you, try to be curious.

I want to be clear here: I am discussing over-involvement, habitually, in high-intensity drama that you have the choice to avoid. This is not the same as being party to tragic events or misfortune that may have occurred in your life and were beyond your control. You will know the difference.

AVOIDANCE

When life is filled with high-intensity drama a lot of the time, it creates a reason to disengage from other parts of life. It also provides the perfect excuse to disengage from people, situations or circumstances that you may want to avoid. This can sound something like:

- I can't, I'm so terribly busy.
- I had such a horrendous experience last time, I won't do that again.
- Anything that can go wrong, will go wrong for me.
- It's just all too much for me to cope with.

The absorption in drama, whatever the drama is, gives you permission to use avoidant strategies to opt out of an unappealing aspect of your life.

COMPENSATORY MECHANISMS

Most excessive behaviours are over-compensating for a sense that something is lacking in your life. For example, you might repeatedly get involved in situations that you know are wrong for you. This could be linked to an underlying lack of confidence or self-belief that you find hard to admit. The dramatic situations help make up for that. The onus is never on you and the problem gets immersed in some sort of high drama.

ATTENTION-SEEKING

Earlier I talked about centre-stage roles and how attractive they can be as they lead to attention and applause. Sometimes you will use excessive drama to take the centre-stage role in life. It could be that whatever drama pattern you strongly identify with gets you more of something: attention, sympathy, applause or adulation. The list is endless. You are in the limelight short term but suffer longer term as these behaviours stop you moving forward in a helpful way. They are not sustainable and don't address the underlying issues.

CONSTRUCTED IDENTITY

This can happen when your personal identity gets closely associated with high-intensity dramatic events. It could sound like:

- This could only happen to me.
- Things always go wrong when I'm around.

- I attract the drama.
- I'm doomed; I'm a disaster.

Part of personal identity gets caught up in dramatic narratives you create. You then start to believe this is the role you should play in life or that this is what people expect of you.

HEREDITARY PATTERNS

Sometimes you become what you have observed. If you have witnessed over-involvement in drama or drama-seeking behaviours in your family during your formative years, then this can become normalized. Breaking unhealthy patterns that don't serve you well is important here. Often you may have to let go of familial patterns that don't work for you in your adult life. Many families have patterns of drama interweaved into the dynamic. The skill is being able to step out of this (which I will come to now).

HOW TO BREAK THE CYCLE OF DRAMA ADDICTION

Sean is a thirty-five-year-old banker, who really struggled with finding a meaningful relationship. He described a catalogue of failed relationships in which he was cheated on, lied to, manipulated, robbed and blackmailed. His story sounded like a dramatic movie, in which he was the victim of many women. He cried in a session after reminiscing that he regularly felt 'f*cked over by women'. He told me he had chosen a male therapist to avoid being messed around by another woman!

When I started to explore each of the relationship break-ups, I discovered that none of the narratives were actually true. He was suspicious that one partner was having an affair, so he ended the relationship. He wasn't sure that he was robbed but he accused the next girlfriend of stealing a watch. He was never blackmailed but felt threatened when the next girlfriend shared that she had told her father about some of his insecurities. He had written dramatic scripts that were highly exaggerated versions of reality that allowed him to escape intimacy or commitment.

Sean didn't meet the criteria for any specific psychiatric disorder and had clear insight into his 'paranoid notions'. In therapy he realized these were exaggerated stories that got him out of relationships. He admitted he knew the stories weren't fully true but he was able to convince himself using partial evidence that served the purpose of allowing him to opt out of relationships. He would then get lots of support from friends, which he enjoyed. He also acknowledged enjoying the extremity of emotions that each new scenario would bring. As he put it, 'It's like living in a movie.'

He was hooked on creating dramas that stopped him having relationships. Further exploration uncovered his real issue with women was linked to a very complex relationship with his mother. Sean's way of managing this was getting caught up in a cycle of dramatic constructed narratives that allowed him to run away every time he felt close to a female.

I know this example might read as extreme in nature but you may have variations of your own in different circumstances.

I suggest a four-step method for breaking the pattern of drama addiction:

1. **Admitting** that you are engaged in a highly exaggerated habitual response to life events (drama behaviours).
2. **Naming** the drama patterns you engage with and starting to manage them, one at a time.
3. **Replacing** drama patterns with healthier strategies.
4. Offering a **non-judgemental** approach to yourself when engaging with this work.

ADMITTING

This is not an easy step because you now consciously know this is something you have to take responsibility for. When I work with clients who are very hooked on drama they initially respond in different ways to the suggestion, ranging from being defensive or apologetic to feeling embarrassed. This is understandable – put simply it is part of being human and just another way of dealing with life. Remember this is not the full story and doesn't define you but it could be a significant contributory factor to your unhappiness.

It's a big deal to admit that you are contributing to or creating some of the problems in your own life by over-engaging with drama. This takes a lot of guts and courage. This first step will immediately set up new foundations for you so that when you fall into the 'drama trap' you can regain control and opt for alternatives (which is one of the next steps). However you decide to admit this drama pattern, addiction or choice (call it what you want) is entirely your call. You could decide to write it down, share with a close friend or even talk it over with a therapist if that would be helpful for you.

I heard it declared very eloquently and humorously by a client who said, 'My sh*t is that I'm a drama queen and I never knew it.'

NAMING

This relates to some of the drama traits I mentioned earlier in the chapter. I would encourage you to read over these patterns again (now you have more insight) and name what you identify with. There is a useful expression in therapy that when you name something, you own it. I think this is true.

Try to be as specific as you can about the key areas in which you notice drama move into your life. This will help you identify patterns quickly when they come up.

REPLACING

My guidance here is broad as your patterns are going to be very personal. But try to replace drama involvement, drama-seeking and drama addiction with behaviours that are adaptive. A useful way of judging whether your behaviours are adaptive in any given circumstance is to ask yourself whether your actions or responses feel:

- **Balanced.** Does your response or action feel measured, balanced and not exaggerated?
- **Regulated emotionally.** Are you seeking thrills, highs or intensity for the sake of it?
- **Helpful.** Does your action or response create difficulties or unnecessary challenges for you?
- **Self-aware.** Based on our work, ask yourself if you are compensating, seeking attention or avoiding something via the drama route.

NON-JUDGEMENT

It's worth remembering that if you start judging or beating yourself up while doing this part of the work, it has the potential to become a substitute internal drama. You are simply learning about your behaviour. When letting go of drama patterns you are deciding to remove a potential barrier to your happiness. You haven't done anything wrong. You are simply moving on from a way of behaving that doesn't stand you well any more.

HOW THIS WILL CONTRIBUTE TO YOUR HAPPINESS

Anyone I've worked with who reports dramatic, highly exaggerated responses or actions in their life also reports feeling exhausted a lot of the time. Likewise, performers of any description report feeling tired after a show (after the initial performance high). This is to be expected as excessive levels of chemicals such as adrenaline and cortisol will have been released during the 'act'. The exhaustion experienced afterwards is the mind and body's compensatory mechanism to try to restore balance after a surge of activity.

Letting go of drama is opting in for a more balanced approach to life. It's a new pattern not based on excessive highs, intensity, conflicts, chemical rushes or maladaptive strategies for managing life. The benefits for your life are therefore significant and include:

- Regulated emotional state
- Balanced chemical state (as described previously)
- Clearer thinking as you allow the rational part of your brain (pre-frontal cortex) to operate more efficiently
- Improvement in relationships as you will be less prone to conflict
- Healthier perspective on life as processing will be more fact-based and rational
- Improved overall wellbeing (excessive drama induces stress responses so a reduction in this has a positive physical and psychological impact).

COMMITMENT

Like most of the other work in the book, commitment when managing drama patterns is a daily requirement. It involves unlearning a particular way of acting or responding to life so it will take practice. Staying curious about this will enable you to observe your daily behaviour dispassionately, acknowledge it as drama-seeking, then alter your response. Each time you do this, you help change a pattern. In time, a more balanced response becomes the new norm.

A useful tool for this commitment is keeping a graph of your daily drama patterns, rating them one to ten (one being no drama, ten being high drama). Make a note each day of what contributed to these drama moments and it will help you identify any traps you might fall into. It then makes it easier to avoid these traps in the future.

CASE STUDY

Life stories of some of the world's iconic stars have featured on our movie screens lately: Elton John, Freddie Mercury, Judy Garland and Tina Turner, to name but a few.

Each story is filled with heartache, pain and some very tragic events happening to people of immense talent.

Each story is also filled with intense drama, part of the reason why they have been box office hits!

Throughout each of the life stories we witness extreme highs, lows, applause, adulation, conflicts, fast-paced lives and histrionic outbursts. Drama is abundant in all of their lives, internal and external, and at some stage they all recognize that it's contributing to their unhappiness. In the end, they all seek change.

The drama isn't always related to unfortunate external events; it's also linked to choices made by the individuals as they navigate life. The drama patterns we observe serve a purpose: they distract them, compensate for what they perceive they lack and help them to cope. What we learn is that it doesn't bring happiness, and ultimately they all discover that at some point in their stories.

I say this without judgement, rather with admiration. Each life story shares a legacy and leaves the viewer with several messages, an important one being that you often need to let go of possessions, harmful attitudes such as holding on to drama, a destructive way of life, even people – all those things you use to mask your pain – to find happiness.

Maybe now is the time to re-write the script for the movie of *your* life. Drama doesn't always bring happiness. More often it creates distraction and distress. You have the power to edit this. Some questions to ponder:

- How would you like to be remembered?
- What legacy do you want to leave behind?
- How dramatic is your story and is it bringing you the happiness you desire?

SUMMARY

- Drama patterns can impact negatively on your life.
- Patterns can always be explained by underlying psychological processes.
- Drama patterns can be broken by admitting, naming, replacing and managing them without judgement.
- Dealing with this will have a positive impact on your life, your wellbeing and your happiness.

CHAPTER 10

LIVING IN THE NOW

I started this book talking about the importance of letting go of the past. I want to finish with an appeal: to achieve true happiness, consider prising yourself away from future-gazing too.

The future is the one thing many people become fixated on as the route to happiness. They plan, predict, hope, obsess, and desperately try to control it. When they do so, the present moment often gets lost, as does, ironically, any chance of happiness!

How often do you tell yourself that you will be happier in the future when you have something, achieve something, arrive . . . and on and on it goes. An endless state of dissatisfaction and unhappiness hoping that the future holds the answers to what you seek now.

Before starting this chapter, I decided to stop and go for a walk to one of my favourite places of inspiration.

When I arrived there, I was the only person around as it was near closing time. Thoroughly enjoying the space and anonymity, I wandered aimlessly. I browsed the various tombstones, curious about the hundreds of people laid to rest.

Yes, I went to a graveyard to seek inspiration!

You might be questioning my sanity or be wary of my weirdness but I can explain.

Death is a certainty in life. A walk in a graveyard didn't make me feel sad (don't worry, this doesn't get morose). As I meandered along the pathway, I found wisdom in knowing that every person buried in the graveyard had navigated their way through life and dealt with the many issues we all face day-to-day. I got distracted by a headstone that read, 'He found happiness in simplicity.'

I suddenly felt the deepest connection and understanding with this stranger.

As I continued to wander through the graveyard, I noticed that not a single tombstone mentioned:

- How successful a person was
- How much money they made
- How famous they were
- How popular they were
- How amazingly fit they were
- How talented they were
- What colour, race, sexuality or religion they were
- What mistakes they made
- Or how many followers they had on Twitter!

However, almost every tombstone did include details of the following:

- How much the person would be missed
- Names of people who loved them
- The values the person lived by
- Spiritual hopes they had
- Gratitude for their life
- How they would always be remembered.

I also noticed that the words peace, love and thankful were abundant on many tombstones.

Every one of the lives in this graveyard had a story to tell, from the infant leaving heartbroken parents behind or the teenager who didn't make it to his eighteenth birthday party to the one-hundred-year-old who had lived through two world wars. Each lived through life's trials and tribulations and in the end, the only thing that they would be remembered for – the only truly important thing – was the impact they had on the people closest to them. They weren't being remembered for any of the things in our future we tend to spend time worrying about, and which, in many cases, we can't control: when they'd chosen to retire, what schools their children had been accepted into or how many promotions they'd had.

I've seen many people struggle with the notion of letting go of the future. Buddhists often emphasize the importance of accepting that nothing is permanent, and living more in the here and now as a path to greater happiness. It's my belief that we try to control our future by planning it, wishing it away and filling it with as much as possible because we cannot accept our own mortality – that we, and everyone we know, will inevitably die one day. Thinking about and planning for the future to remove any possibility of a negative outcome lulls us into believing that we control what happens to us, eases the pain of accepting that nothing is for ever, including life, and distracts us from the truth.

I think it is this preoccupation with controlling our futures that leads to much unhappiness because it stops us from noticing all the many reasons for joy and wonder that exist around us in the present moment. Ultimately, I think for most people this is linked to the realization that everything is impermanent.

I have something to confess. In my late twenties I went to see a fortune-teller, desperate to hear what the future might hold for me. I wasn't unhappy at the time but I was curious about my future direction.

I went with a friend who decided to go in first. When she came out after her reading, she looked bemused. It was later I discovered that she had been told that she would have three children (she is infertile), that she would marry a very rich man (she is gay) and that her parents would start a new business in the fashion industry (they are farmers in Ireland).

My reading was equally interesting. I was told that I would return to my Scottish roots within the year (I'm Irish), I would pursue a lifelong ambition of learning to play a musical instrument (I went to music school for eight years as a teenager) and that the woman of my dreams wasn't a blonde lady but a brunette (need I say more on this?).

The fortune-teller revealed nothing of value, and even if she had, how would it have helped me? It wouldn't stop what was coming next. Of course, there is very little we can be absolutely certain about in life and here we come to the heart of the issue.

On that note, our next stop is looking in more detail at why you might struggle to let go of the future. I won't offer any Mystic Meg guidance here but hopefully some insights that help you understand yourself more and navigate your way to happiness.

WHY YOU CAN'T LET GO OF THE FUTURE

It would be foolish of me to suggest that you can completely let go of every aspect of the future and live in an eternal state of 'oneness'. Your mind, your patterns and the ever-changing landscape of life won't allow it. Even monks who live in secluded conditions with no responsibility describe struggling with future concerns.

Some degree of forward planning is always necessary in life otherwise you wouldn't grow, develop or move forward. Imagine a world where people didn't look to the future. We would remain stuck in a place of no progress. But this isn't the problem.

Challenges occur when you consciously spend a lot of time trying to control the aspects of the future that are fundamentally out of your control. You can of course try to influence some elements of your life but ultimately you can't control precisely:

- How long you or other people will live
- Whether other people will always be well
- If and when you will have children
- If and when you will meet someone and fall in love
- What will happen next
- How other people behave
- Natural disasters
- Atrocities
- Outcomes of varying situations
- A predictable trajectory for your entire life.

THERE WILL *ALWAYS* BE VARIABLES OUTSIDE OF YOUR CONTROL OR POWER

Have you ever watched a duck trying to swim against the natural current of a river? It gets bounced around, looks confused, gets separated from the others, and ultimately exhausts itself; the current is always stronger. And this is true of the flow of life.

Learning to go more with the natural flow of life leads to more ease and a smoother journey, and it lessens the burden of trying to control everything that happens.

I believe letting go of the future doesn't mean you can't plan or hope for a future but it does mean you need to let go of those things that aren't controllable. This involves learning to accept the uncertainty of many parts of life! I know this is tough but it's an option that will bring you much relief.

If you struggle to relinquish apparent control on the future, you may well perceive life as:

- Disappointing you
- Frustrating you
- Robbing you of power
- Conflicting with what you want

- Persecuting you

This is an uncomfortable way to live and will certainly be making you unhappy.

You will at this stage know that all behaviours arise as a result of underlying psychological processes and understanding this is crucial. This is true of struggling to let go of controlling the future. In my experience, there are four major mechanisms at work here:

1. Fear of the future
2. Intolerance of not knowing
3. Angst around mortality
4. Ego states

FEAR OF THE FUTURE

Fear is probably one of the most powerful human emotions. It is driven by our threat system (the brain mechanism that protects us), and when activated it is a force to be reckoned with. When you are frightened of something in the future, your instincts can send you in a few directions as you might try to:

- Run away from the future

- Protect yourself from it
- Prepare yourself for it
- Defend yourself from it
- Stop it happening

Living in a world that is filled with threat and unpredictability (politically, socially, economically and personally), it's not surprising that we try to manage the future. There is a problem though. Often fear-driven instinct takes up a lot of energy and exhausts your personal resources. Your internal voice may be telling you that trying to control the future is the right thing, that controlling it will reduce your fear and keep you safe, but often it doesn't. Remember, this isn't about situations when a fear-driven response might be healthy, e.g. if you were running away from a dangerous situation. This is living in a perpetual state of trying to control or pre-empt the future in some way. You will be left depleted and feeling powerless. You will also miss many positive parts of the life you have now.

INTOLERANCE OF NOT KNOWING

Earlier, in the chapter on worry, you may remember the definition of anxiety as an 'intolerance of uncertainty'. I think when you become excessively focussed on the future, it relates closely to worry. It is the worry of not knowing what's coming next.

If you don't have concrete guarantees on what the future will bring, the brain can trick you into believing you can regain control by planning, predicting or worrying about the future. This becomes a means of managing the discomfort of not knowing.

When I discuss this with clients who are preoccupied with the future, they often look alarmed at first. The thought of dropping the safety net of future-focussed concerns is new territory. But it's beneficial in the long run.

I overheard a fascinating conversation on a train a few months back between an elderly father and his son. The father was likely in his late seventies and the son late thirties. The son was discussing various aspects of his life with his father. His new mortgage, savings, university plans for his children, savings accounts for his children's weddings and so on.

I could hear the son was anxious and absorbed in future worries and planning. The father listened intently to his son for at least fifteen minutes, and then asked, 'How is life at the moment?' The son paused, and responded, 'What do you mean?' His father then asked, 'How are the kids enjoying school? How is Susie [the man's wife, I assumed] enjoying the new job?' There was another pause, and it was clear the son was struggling to answer. He didn't really know. He had gotten so caught up in the future.

I was intrigued listening to this conversation, when suddenly the father said, 'Be careful, son. You're missing the best moments.'

Let me put a question to you. Are you missing the best moments? If so, you have an opportunity now to rethink and weigh up whether living in the future really serves you as well as you think.

ANGST AROUND MORTALITY

My motivation to become a psychotherapist was influenced by this topic. I worked in the field of palliative care, in my early career. In this area of care, there are often discussions about 'psychological pain' as clients face their own death. Research shows that physical symptoms worsen with increased psychological distress, often linked to fear of dying or some angst about mortality.

Many studies by Buddhists, philosophers, existential writers and psychologists show that mortality creates distress for some people leading to questions such as 'What's it all about?', 'What the purpose of life?' and 'What's my purpose?' Again, the not knowing the answers to some of the great mysteries around life and death creates discomfort in the here and now. The escape to the future can be used as a way of avoiding this or trying to find answers somewhere in the future.

Ironically, much of the research in this area informs us that many people find more meaning and peace by living in the here and now.

EGO STATES

Each of us has ego states. These states consist of how we think, feel and behave, making up our personality. Some aspects of these states can sometimes be a little uncomfortable to acknowledge. For example, if we have a need to be in control a lot of the time this might create challenges in an uncertain world. However, they are part of being human. I once had a supervisor who would joke about keeping an eye on the dictator within, who was out to take control of everything!

A major contributor to our egos is our need to be in control – to know, to manage, to take charge, to conquer, to succeed.

When it comes to living in the future, the ego can try to take a lead as the hero who holds it all together. Our egos will attempt to manage our destiny and captain all of life's trials.

Awareness of this is important because sometimes your ego state may not want to relinquish control of beliefs such as:

- I know better.
- I must hold on to keeping it all together.
- I don't trust that things will work out.
- I need to be in charge.

I guess the ego can be a little like a pompous well-meaning friend who believes they know better about most things, when sometimes they might just need to accept that they don't, and they can't be in charge of everything around them.

HOW TO LET GO OF LIVING IN THE FUTURE

Unlike previous chapters when I have taken a more prescriptive route, I am going to take a simpler route here. I am going the mindfulness way.

I think mindfulness has become a little more complicated of late than it needs to be. For me, the premise is simple. It is learning to become more present in your life, here and now. Whatever you decide to bring a deeper awareness to, and truly notice, is OK, and can be accepted without judgement.

How you bring attention to the here and now is entirely up to you. It could be paying attention to drinking a cup of tea, tasting, smelling, savouring the moment. That's meditating, that's mindfulness. It's a single point of focus on one thing at a given time.

It could be a walk in which you stay focussed on your walk as you absorb everything you see, hear, feel and touch.

It could be staring at the sky, watching your breath rise and fall, or listening to the sound of the sea.

On a broader level mindfulness is about showing up – mentally as well as physically – in your everyday life. Instead of focussing on the future, it's about becoming more engaged in the 'now'. That involves experiencing more, listening more, looking more, feeling more, and being more engaged in the life you have now.

As simplistic as it sounds, this is where your power will be found – in the now. Much of the energy spent focussing on the future is wasted time. Most of what you need is right in front of you at this moment in time. The challenge is giving yourself permission to come out of the future (and the past) and step into what you have in this very moment. It's no more complicated than that.

Living this way will bring you more peace and happiness than you can imagine. I know this, not just as a therapist, but also as someone who wasted many years living in the future; nothing I sought was there.

HOW THIS WILL CONTRIBUTE TO YOUR HAPPINESS

You may remember from earlier in the book that there are thousands of studies reporting on the benefits of living in the present moment. The studies not only report improvements in overall wellbeing and state of mind, but also in brain functionality.

Letting go of future-based living will have significant positive impact on your life. These are the improvements, based on my experience, that you will discover:

- A sense of having fewer burdens as you focus on managing what is happening in the here and now, rather than trying to manage events in both the present and the future.

- Reduced anxiety – future-based worries lead to overthinking, so reducing these will in turn make you feel less anxious.
- Improvements in your mood – taking your focus off the future will allow you to experience more of the here and now, which, studies show, has a positive impact on mood.
- Improvements in concentration, creativity, productivity, and memory from freeing up space in your brain.
- Renewed appreciation and gratitude for what you have in your life at the moment.
- More of an awareness of what is going on in your life right now. This allows you to make better decisions when it comes to making helpful changes in your life.

COMMITMENT

If you have spent a long time living in future-mode, this will all feel rather strange and unusual. Commitment for this part of our work is focussed on turning up more for your life in the here and now. In short, you are giving yourself permission to live fully, rather than in a state of preoccupation, worrying about something yet to come.

You will fail sometimes and get it wrong. There will be days when it feels tough, but these are the days when you will learn most, as is true of most of life.

Some ways in which you might achieve this are:

- Stop a few times in the day to check in with how you are in the moment. It will ground you.
- Schedule 'catch a breath moments' in your day when you take time out to simply breathe. It will take your attention away from the future.
- Practise letting go of future-focussed living.
- Become more focussed on experiencing fully everyday moments, even the simple things like drinking a cup of tea. It brings focus to the here and now.

CASE STUDY

When I worked in the field of palliative care, I had a major wake-up call around the volume of time I spent living in the future. I spoke earlier in the book about the wisdom that comes from working with people who are dying. I want to close this book by sharing their wisdom on the future.

This isn't a single case study. It is the voices of hundreds of people I had the privilege of looking after in their final days.

The interesting thing about working with people who are dying is that they often cut quickly through the BS. It's incredibly refreshing!

Molly was one such character. When she discovered she was dying, she booked herself onto a luxury cruise liner. She left her husband and family a note saying,

'I need some me time and there's milk in the fridge!' Then off she went. I received a picture of her at the captain's party, glass of champagne in hand, with a caption, 'This is my time.'

When she returned, we laughed at her adventure. She had, for the first time, put her own needs first and allowed herself to live. Despite facing death, she opted out of fixating on the future.

And this is your time too! But how much of your life are you truly living?

I'd like to share with you the ten lessons these people, whose deaths were imminent, taught me about the future. These alone, if heeded, could, I believe, make us all ten times happier:

- The only guarantees you have are now. Don't waste too much time worrying about the future.
- Look for the joy in everyday things.

- Time with people is precious. Use it well now.
- Most things work themselves out in the end.
- Worrying about the future stops you enjoying what you have now.
- Follow the path that makes you passionate. Don't wait until tomorrow.
- Everything you need is within you.
- Make every moment count.
- Be grateful for everything life offers you.
- This is your time.

You can't be blissfully happy all the time of course. Life isn't a fairy tale. But I wholeheartedly believe you can be ten times happier than you might be currently.

You have an incredible opportunity, right now, to make some significant changes that will help you get there.

Thank you for allowing me the privilege of coming with you on the start of your journey. I'm rooting for you all of the way.

CHAPTER 11

RESETTING AFTER TOUGH TIMES

One of the most important parts of my job is teaching a client how to recover after tough times. We all know that life sometimes delivers the unexpected and no matter how 'balanced' we are, we can suddenly feel as if we have been flung off a horse at a rodeo! This chapter is about learning how to get back up, reset and move forward when the proverbial hits the fan. At the time of writing, it's exactly a year since Covid-19 swept the globe. I think most of us would agree that this has been a hellish time. We have regularly been engulfed with worrying headlines and, for many, experiences of illness, death, loss, uncertainty and hardship. Daily life has delivered a darker new reality. For many people, it has been the hardest of times. It has been a *traumatic time*. And for me this is a crucial point. Tough times often come with some degree of trauma that may get minimised or ignored. In this chapter I will explore tough times through the lens of trauma, no matter how big or small the event. True recovery can begin only when we allow ourselves to deal with what's happened. Focusing on trauma does just that; it allows space to deal with the event. While this chapter is motivated by the impact of a pandemic, that is not the central focus. The chapter is relevant for all areas of life. It is a roadmap for getting you back on track when you feel as if everything has gone wrong. Admittedly, working though trauma isn't easy; it takes effort and will feel challenging at times. And no, nothing worthwhile is ever easy, but the benefits are indisputable. I promise that, step by step, you will start to feel better. In the following pages, we will explore in more detail why we struggle or get 'stuck' in tough times, how to move forward, the benefits for your life and what's needed of you. How we recover during times of adversity is ultimately determined by how we respond. The event is just the trigger.

Everything else is linked to how our internal processes deal with what's going on.

DEFINE TOUGH TIMES AND UNDERSTAND TRAUMA

All of life comes to a therapy room, and if the walls could talk, we'd hear about: loss, bereavement, break-ups and relationship problems, redundancy and work issues, bullying, hardship and health issues. The list is endless.

I believe that there are two types of trauma: 'tall T trauma' and 'small t trauma'. When someone has been through a tall T trauma it's possible that they might then experience PTSD (Post-Traumatic Stress Disorder). Symptoms for this range from flashbacks, intrusions (mentally re-experiencing the event) and nightmares to feeling highly anxious or avoiding situations that trigger memories. These can feel debilitating and make functioning day to day a big challenge. The pain of PTSD is unimaginable to those who don't understand it and such a level of trauma requires professional support. While I give some pointers in this chapter, if you feel that you have PTSD, then undoubtedly further face-to-face support will be needed. Please don't hesitate to talk to your doctor or a professional for guidance. Here my focus will primarily be small t traumas that create tough times. Small t trauma also creates distress, but not at the same level as tall T trauma. There may be a few milder symptoms of PTSD, but more obvious changes will likely be visible with mood, motivation and anxiety. When I meet people in therapy, I often see lots of small t traumas that have been ignored. Unsurprisingly this is often the root of their symptoms, and they need to be dealt with. When you don't process a difficult period in your life, the unprocessed material can contribute to some of the psychological symptoms you experience. It is also part of the reason why you might be struggling to pick yourself up. Many people feel that it is easier to avoid, numb or ignore the uncomfortable traumatic times in life. In the short term the avoidance creates relief, but in the longer term the issues accumulate.

Whatever it is you're struggling with in your life at the moment, I'm sorry you are having a difficult time. I can't wave a magic wand and make your problem disappear, but together we can make sense of your experience and help you come through it stronger.

WHY YOU GET STUCK IN TOUGH TIMES

In my experience, no matter how awful the circumstance or events, people respond differently in dark times. I remember speaking to 85-year-old Derek who had survived fighting in the Second World War, PTSD, bankruptcy and cancer, to name but a few. After his wife died last year, he 'emotionally collapsed', wondering if he would ever get up again. He eventually found his way back. Derek was clearly grieving for his wife, but there were other factors aggravating his pain. His wife had died suddenly and Derek had attempted to resuscitate her. He believed he'd 'failed' her when she was pronounced dead. Several months later, he began experiencing some mild trauma symptoms consisting of intrusive images of the event and replaying details, while partially blaming himself for her death. Consequently, he was withdrawing from life, drinking every night and showing signs of depression. His grief was the trigger for his pain, but he wasn't processing any of his loss. His response to the event wasn't allowing him to deal with the trauma, and so he couldn't heal and learn to adapt to life without his wife.

How many of the following ways of 'thinking' do you relate to as you deal with the traumatic periods in your own life?

- This shouldn't be happening, I can't accept this
- Bad things always happen to me
- I have no control over how I deal with this
- This is so unfair
- Why is this happening?
- I can't deal with this
- I'm weak and powerless
- Maybe it's all my fault?

How many of the following behaviours do you identify with during traumatic periods?

- Socially withdrawing
- Angry outbursts
- Dropping routines
- Disengaging from work, hobbies, interests
- Increased eating, alcohol or drug use or other substances
- Over-engaging with negative content on TV/social media/radio
- Disconnecting from talking about feelings
- Endlessly worrying or overthinking

- Treating yourself unkindly
- Hypervigilance to situations that make you feel unsafe?

And, of course, we can't exclude the following feelings during traumatic periods that you may experience:

- Sadness
- Anxiety
- Panic
- Confusion
- Numbness
- Despair
- Fear
- Loneliness

I encourage you to make a note here of the symptoms you're experiencing as it's important to be able to look at this truthfully. The lists here are not exhaustive, so you may have some of your own to add.

I'm confident that if you identify with any (or all) of the thoughts, behaviours and emotions on the list, it's time for you to stop, reset and recover.

I believe there are four key psychological reasons (besides the life event you have experienced) that will help explain obstacles to your recovery:

1. Trauma has never been fully processed
2. You are not prioritising self-care/self-compassion
3. Denying the aftermath of trauma
4. You are self-sabotaging your own recovery

I appreciate that this might sound prescriptive, but I know it's true. Life events have many narratives, but human responses tend to be familiar in the face of suffering.

1. TRAUMA HAS NEVER BEEN FULLY PROCESSED

When we experience a traumatic event and it isn't processed (dealt with) properly, the memory stays active on the right-hand side of the brain in an unhelpful way, creating symptoms such as severe anxiety, depression, flashbacks, intrusions, hypervigilance and avoidance. These are the symptoms of PTSD (tall T trauma). The aim of treatment is to process the memory so that it moves to the hippocampus on the left-hand side of the brain. This enables the memory to be filed away in a safe place, leading to a reduction in symptoms. In short, this will mean that the trauma has been processed. It's important to know that a similar process can take place with small t traumas. The symptoms of PTSD may not be as acute, but the residual anxiety and symptoms of depression are. Unless you pay attention to the underlying maintenance of anxiety and/or depression (i.e. trauma), the symptoms will keep coming back.

2. NOT PRIORITISING SELF-CARE/SELF-COMPASSION

We live in a world where there seems to be an expectation that we 'keep calm and carry on', even in the hardest of times. Similarly, there are views everywhere that self-care is a little self-indulgent or 'fluffy'. Compromising self-care and self-compassion comes with great risk because they are the foundations for stability and recovery. When we fail to look after our mental wellbeing, we suffer more. When we fail to be compassionate to ourselves, we delay recovery.

Can you imagine having major surgery and expecting to continue as normal directly afterwards? Of course you can't. There would be a period of rest, recovery, time out of work, adjustments, medical appointments and a general need to take care of yourself. All of this would be necessary to enable recovery from the surgery. It's similar with emotional wounds after a traumatic time. But most don't prioritise care in the same way. We carry on as normal, minimising pain and believing that it will somehow magic itself away.

It will come as no surprise that that's never the case.

3. DENYING THE AFTERMATH OF TRAUMA

I would be rich if I had a penny for each time I heard someone say:

- I'm OK, it's no big deal
- There are people worse off than I am
- I don't want to make a fuss
- I don't need any help
- It's not so bad
- I get by
- It's just one of those things

The reality is, it's hard for most of us to be vulnerable and accept that life hasn't been going so well. It is difficult to say, 'I'm not coping' or 'I'm struggling'. I hear people regularly say that they fear rejection or worry they will be seen as weak if they admit vulnerability. So, they opt for denial and pretend to cope. Unfortunately, this comes at a cost for mental wellness.

The denial of uncomfortable feelings that tend to come after traumatic times creates a whirlwind of internal conflict. A battle occurs between covering up what's going on while trying to function 'normally'. The problem here is that emotions begin to 'backlog'. In time they accumulate and eventually erupt like a volcano!

Denial is a form of repression that tries to bury difficult emotional experiences. The problem is that emotions have a strong charge and tend not to give up until they have been dealt with. Short-term denial creates some ease; in the longer term it breeds a host of other psychological issues. It's almost as if the emotions persevere to create a sense of discomfort that eventually forces us to pay attention. So, the next time you are experiencing some negative emotions, it's worth bearing in mind that they could be a wake-up call to pay attention to what's going on within you. Often the way out of difficult times is to go inwards.

4. SELF-SABOTAGE

There is a saboteur within most of us – a part of us that sometimes whispers and screams:

- You're not good enough
- It's your fault
- You don't deserve good things
- You're helpless
- You're unlovable
- You're hopeless

As adults we learn how to manage our saboteur – for the most part. At times of trauma, though, it has the annoying habit of dropping by for a visit. But our saboteur is not a welcomed visitor. It normally comes with a host of unhelpful judgements, opinions and criticisms. It's almost as if our shadow side identifies an opportunity in moments of strife. Being aware of this is essential as it gives you the power to deal with your saboteur.

I heard this articulated brilliantly by a client, Ian, who, after a long period of systemic bullying in his workplace, was made redundant. He subsequently suffered a breakdown. In his darkest moments, he likened his saboteur to Eeyore in *Winnie-the-Pooh*. Thankfully Ian learnt to identify his saboteur and challenge the unhelpful, biased narrative it presented. In time he was able to rewrite a more helpful, self-affirmative script.

HOW TO MOVE FORWARD

Now that you have a greater understanding of the obstacles to resetting and recovery, which can be dealt with both directly and indirectly, it's time to look at the mechanics of moving forward.

There are three focus areas to resetting from a traumatic or difficult time in life:

Dealing with it
Rewriting the story
Resetting and recovery

FOCUS AREA 1: DEALING WITH IT

The expression 'deal with it' can sound harsh. Although not a traumatic event, I remember writing an essay at university and feeling a great sense of satisfaction on completion. It was very short-lived when I discovered I hadn't saved it properly on my computer. After quite a few expletives, head rubbing and several attempts to recover it, I had to reconcile myself to the fact that the essay was gone. The next day, (also submission day) I told my tutor of the lost essay, hoping for a compassionate response. This wasn't the case. A hard stare from him with the words 'Deal with it' was his offering. I was left with a sense of panic that this was my problem and I had to sort it. This, of course, was true to some extent, but some compassion, flexibility, understanding and a little kindness would have helped immensely.

And this is true of ourselves as we try to reset and recover when we are in a tough space. Telling ourselves to just deal with it and move on, won't cut it. Yes, I know there are many gurus out there telling us that 'You've got this' and we need to 'toughen up' or 'move on'. If only our emotions and psychological processes were that simple.

You do, of course, need to deal with whatever has gone on in your life, but it's *how* you deal with it that is the game changer. It can be done in two steps:

STEP 1. ACKNOWLEDGING AND ACCEPTING

There is no sugar-coating the fact that this is never easy. I can recount many, *many* clients recovering from a tough event who say at the start of therapy:

- I will never get over this
- I can't accept it's over
- I can't believe this happened

- I can't live without him/her
- This should never have happened
- I don't want to deal with this
- I don't want to talk about this
- I want to forget about this and talk about something else

The list goes on, but responses are familiar. The solution lies in moving towards acknowledging, accepting and dealing with what has happened.

Acknowledging is allowing yourself to admit that a terrible event has happened. It is recognising that resisting or denying will aggravate your suffering. It is worth remembering that you have survived the event/s, so you can also survive the aftermath. The moment you give yourself permission to do this, it's almost like shining a light on the past event and saying, 'I see you and I'm going to deal with you.' It is the beginning of healing.

Accepting is also equally challenging. No one wants to accept the 'bad' times or awful experiences, especially if they have come with great loss and distress. Accepting a past situation doesn't mean that you are submitting or giving up. It is an act of courage that allows you to deal with your reality as it is, not how you think it *should have been*. It also doesn't mean you become submissive and consciously allow yourself to be treated badly in the here and now. There are times when we know it is right and fitting to walk away from situations, people or circumstances that harm us (if we have been able to do so).

I am reminded of Maggie, a client I treated for PTSD after she'd been severely injured in a terrorist explosion. Not only did she lose her job and her mobility, but she was undoubtedly traumatised, anxious and depressed. Therapy involved encouraging Maggie to voice her rage, frustration and sadness. But she had become stuck on the belief that it 'should never have happened'. This held her in a powerless and hopeless state. While she was right that it should never have happened, the reality was that *it had happened* and living with that reality was intolerable for her.

Through treatment, Maggie was able to set about working on acknowledging and accepting her story. This was the beginning of her resetting and recovering. It took time, patience and a great deal of self-compassion. It was a first step.

STEP 2: SHARING THE STORY

Everyone needs to tell their stories sometimes, particularly in darker periods. It can be cathartic and therapeutic. I encourage you now, in whichever way it feels comfortable, to begin sharing the story of the trauma that you are working through.

If it feels necessary, you might want to do this with a professional. If the distress feels manageable, then you might feel safe to share with someone you trust. Simply tell the story as it is, without judgement. This will create a sense of release and help unblock any 'stuck' areas.

Alternatively, you can write your experience down in a journal, as a story or any other form you prefer (someone I worked with once wrote theirs as a rap). For others, painting, craftwork, recorded voice or songwriting can be creative means of doing this. The key point is that you are bringing the experience out into the light and allowing it to be told. But it doesn't stop there. In the world of psychology, we know that when trying to recover from dark times, the human mind can inadvertently sabotage recovery, particularly if the event is unprocessed. This normally plays out as a series of unhelpful beliefs or biased, unkind interpretations around what's happened. In short, when telling the story, you might notice a lot of harsh judgements, criticism or even self-blaming coming to the fore. To deal with this, you will likely need to replay and rewrite the events again, but this time with rationality, compassion, self-love and care.

FOCUS AREA 2: REWRITING THE STORY

After acknowledgement, acceptance and telling your story, it often becomes clear how much internal sabotaging goes on. Do any of the following thoughts sound familiar to you:

- Maybe it's my fault
- I should have known better
- I should be over this
- I should have done more
- I feel so guilty
- If only I had…
- Why didn't I see this coming?
- I should have been able to stop this
- I'm so stupid, foolish, naïve
- I deserve this
- I can't be happy again
- I deserve to suffer
- I'm weaker than everyone else
- I'm less able to deal with stuff?

Again, this list could go on, and you may have other thoughts that are destructive and unhelpful.

This is why rewriting the story is crucially important. It's difficult enough working through what you've experienced, but when the voices of judgement, criticism, self-doubt and harshness emerge alongside this, it can feel understandably torturous.

Maggie experienced her self-saboteur a few months after her trauma in the terrorist attack. She critically queried why she had been at the venue at the time of the bomb: 'Why didn't I go at a different time?' She felt guilty that she had survived and others had died. She also felt that she had failed her family after losing her job. She was suffering deeply not only from the impact of the bomb but the explosions in her mind.

I encourage you now to consider going back to telling your story again. Every time you notice that you are 'giving yourself a hard time', replace it with something kinder, flexible, open and compassionate. The reality is, whatever has gone on, you most likely did your best with the information, resources and insights you had at the time. This isn't trying to employ 'magical thinking', but a fair, humane, healing perspective that enables you to reset and recover.

The landscapes of events then begin to look

different as a more hopeful perspective emerges. Rather than self-sabotaging, think of seeing it in some of the ways listed below:

- Despite everything, I managed to cope
- I did my best
- I now know there was nothing I could have done
- This wasn't my fault
- It's incredible I survived this
- I still managed to achieve the following in my life…
- I have learnt so much
- I have more resilience and courage than I realised
- Sometimes bad things happen
- I can grow from this
- I want to reset and recover.

The path is now set for you to reset, recover and, more importantly, reclaim your life.

FOCUS AREA 3: RESETTING AND RECOVERING

We all know what it feels like after a period of physical illness. We are tired, depleted and need convalescent time. It's no different after an episode of psychological or emotional trauma. The human brain, like every other organ in the body, can become worn out and needs time to reset and recover.

Everything we have discussed so far is an integral part of this reset and recovery process, but there are a number of other factors that will support recovery:

- Rest and time out
- Talking to a trusted friend or professional on an ongoing basis
- Evaluating the lessons learned from the time of trauma
- Making adjustments to life that ease everyday pressures
- Surrounding yourself with people who support and understand you
- Making plans for the future that excite you
- Prioritising daily self-care
- Eating well
- Exercising: walking or whatever you can manage (it supports continued processing)
- Considering changes that best support your life

- Practising compassion in your everyday interactions – it will serve as a reminder to be compassionate to yourself.

Above all, remember that you have a right to reclaim your life. It is yours to live.

CASE STUDY – A TOUGH TIME IN MY LIFE

There have been several periods of challenge in my life over the decades (let's not focus too much on how many years that spans). But one period that stands out is the aftermath of my mother's death. She had been ill with cancer for a number of years. In the final stages of her young life, I was very embroiled with a lot of the medical aspects of her care. Then she died. Suddenly I had nothing to occupy my mind. I was left with a sense of emptiness and numbness accompanied by the most overwhelming waves of sadness. But it wasn't just grief. There were also different degrees of trauma from many harrowing memories of watching someone I loved suffer – and not being able to save them (not dissimilar to Derek, as mentioned earlier). I had to deal with this.

A few months later, I was standing in a bar with a few friends who were merrily singing and dancing. It was unbearable for me to be there as I was engulfed with sadness. I made a polite excuse and left. In the back seat of the cab on the way home, I remember discreetly crying and thinking to myself, 'I'm not sure I will ever laugh properly again.' While I was in the depths of sadness and grief, I was equally impatiently trying to 'fix' myself and get back to the frivolities of life. It was as if I was desperate for it to be summer when the reality was winter.

Over the course of many months, a combination of accepting, talking, accommodating the loss and adjusting through this tough period, topped up with a lot of self-care – exercise, walks, meditating – finally enabled me to reset. I was intuitively doing what the psychology research around trauma suggests, even though I hadn't trained in trauma at that point. Life slowly came back. It wasn't instantaneous or a euphoric reawakening but gradually lightness

> emerged. My shoulders dropped, my head lifted and a spark returned somewhere inside. I noticed that I was singing in the shower again and I started to make plans that excited me. My recovery serves as a reminder that we often know what we need to do. The challenge for most of us is translating knowing into doing.

HOW DARK PERIODS CAN IMPROVE YOUR LIFE

I know personally and professionally that dark periods of life can feel overwhelming and never-ending. Sometimes life can deal raw, cruel cards that we can't explain or comprehend. It's the unthinkable, the unimaginable, the devastating moments that throw us off track. It's bad things happening to good people that we can't make sense of.

I can't answer why things sometimes go wrong. But I know with absolute confidence that dark, traumatic times can teach and strengthen us — if we allow them.

It's about learning to work through the dark times to find the light. It's about resetting and recovery, acknowledging and accepting. It's a willingness to show up, trusting the process that we have worked through. If today you are not feeling hopeful, hold on to hope that tomorrow may be a better day. I know that to be true.

Happiness is always possible again. In the times when you feel like you are falling apart, you are simply rebuilding. In the words of the great songwriter Leonard Cohen, 'There's a crack, a crack in everything, that's how the light gets in.'

May you reset – May you recover – May you know – Life comes back.

EPILOGUE

IT TAKES WORK BUT IT'S WORTH IT

I want to wrap up *Ten Times Happier* by sharing truthfully with you my experience of writing a book on happiness. I think people have a notion that therapists, self-help writers or 'gurus' of any description (I don't consider myself a guru, by the way!) live in a state of bliss. Of course, I don't but most of the time I'm happy with my life and myself. And that's simply because I genuinely live what I preach. I work at being happy and that makes the world of difference to my life. If I didn't live the principles of the ten chapters, I know I'd be less happy (maybe ten times less happy).

I promised at the start this wouldn't be a magical

thinking book on happiness. Happiness takes work, and there isn't a shortcut or quick fix. It's a commitment to a particular way of life.

One day, while writing this book, I spoke with my father on the phone. I'd had a bad day, was dosed with a cold and was generally feeling a little grumpy. I became a little irritated with Dad as he updated me on all the latest deaths, illnesses and local gossip. I told him I was tired and didn't want to hear all the bad news stories. He teased me, 'And I thought you were the happy book man!'

I immediately felt irritated and had an irrational moment of questioning my writing a book on happiness whilst I was feeling grumpy.

Troubled by this feeling, I discussed it with my own therapist (part of my professional responsibility is to be in therapy). My therapist looked bemused and asked me if I knew anyone who was 100 per cent happy all the time? Of course, I couldn't think of anyone. He laughed. 'So this book is written by a therapist who also knows what it is to be human?' Indeed, he was right. I do know what it is to be human and I know that happiness takes work.

I won't lie. In an ideal world, I wanted the period of writing this book to be filled with idyllic, happy, peaceful times. But it wasn't. I went to the Cotswolds at one stage for a week staying in a beautiful country cottage. I had visions of the 'happy book writer' sitting by the fire churning out inspirational chapters in a deep state of contentment.

This wasn't the case. During that week my car broke down twice, my dog got ill and it rained persistently for seven days. I also locked myself out of the cottage twice and broke the lock on the door! I was bloody furious and frustrated. But rather than be defeated by this, I did try to practise what I preach and made the best of the situation. I turned around a challenging week and made it a happy, productive week.

Chapter by chapter I unpack the obstacles that get in the way of happiness. Throughout the process of writing this book, I've had to work through each of them in some shape or form.

For example, in the moments of self-doubt I had to let go of the parts of my past that interfere with confidence.

When my aunt recently died unexpectedly, I had to manage a regret that I didn't get to visit her before she died.

In a moment when I got delayed in the process of writing, I had to manage my mind catastrophizing that the book wouldn't be finished on time.

So, life didn't deliver a luxurious portion of happy events all of the time. It delivered life with all its uncertainties, unpredictability, ups and downs, and emotions of every kind. But I was able to deliver the version of myself that enabled me to live happily despite all of this.

And you can too. If you find yourself troubled by things you've said or done in the past, then revisit Chapter 1. If you are fixated on uncertainty concerning the future then Chapter 10 might be a sensible place for you to go. As we all know, managing the mind and the accompanying worries that come and go can be a real challenge, so Chapters 2 and 4 will bring you relief and solutions. If gossip, regular run-ins, interfering behaviour and pot-stirring are getting in the way of your happiness, go back to Chapters 5 and 9. If you recognise yourself in the introduction to Chapter 6, Kick the Habit, then maybe go there.

I hope all of the chapters in the book made sense to you but undoubtedly some chapters will resonate more with you than others. Focus on the chapters that speak most to you and go back over the content as often as you need to. If you noticed your stomach churning when reading a particular chapter or wondered whether I was reading your thoughts, then it's likely this chapter has much for you to take away.

Take the chapters at your own pace.

You might not feel happier straight away. That's OK. But at least you are now doing something about it. That's what's going to make the difference longer term.

But I can promise you that if you start right now, soon you will turn around and look back at the person you are today and barely recognise him/her. You will see how far you've come and you'll realise that you are Ten Times Happier.

I believe that living the 'ten times happier' way will bring you to happier places than you can imagine, even when life throws its curve balls. Maybe now is the time to let go of what's holding you back. This is your life, your time, and you truly deserve to be happy.

May the road rise up to meet you (an old Irish blessing).

For more information and resources from Owen go to:

instagram, twitter @owenokaneten

www.owenokane.com

RESOURCES

MENTAL HEALTH HELPLINES

Whether you're concerned about yourself or a loved one, these helplines and support groups can offer expert advice.

Anxiety UK

Charity providing support if you have been diagnosed with an anxiety condition.

Phone: 03444 775 774 (Monday to Friday, 9.30am to 5.30pm)

Website: www.anxietyuk.org.uk

Bipolar UK

A charity helping people living with manic depression or bipolar disorder.

Website: www.bipolaruk.org.uk

CALM

CALM is the Campaign Against Living Miserably, for men aged 15 to 35.

Phone: 0800 58 58 58 (daily, 5pm to midnight)

Website: www.thecalmzone.net

Men's Health Forum

24/7 stress support for men by text, chat and email.

Website: www.menshealthforum.org.uk

Mental Health Foundation

Provides information and support for anyone with mental health problems or learning disabilities.

Website: www.mentalhealth.org.uk

Mind

Promotes the views and needs of people with mental health problems.

Phone: 0300 123 3393 (Monday to Friday, 9am to 6pm)

Website: www.mind.org.uk

No Panic

Voluntary charity offering support for sufferers of panic attacks and obsessive compulsive disorder (OCD). Offers a course to help overcome your phobia or OCD.

Phone: 0844 967 4848 (daily, 10am to 10pm). Calls cost 5p per minute plus your phone provider's access charge.

Website: www.nopanic.org.uk

OCD Action

Support for people with OCD. Includes information on treatment and online resources.

Phone: 0845 390 6232 (Monday to Friday, 9.30am to 5pm). Calls cost 5p per minute plus your phone provider's access charge

Website: www.ocdaction.org.uk

OCD UK

A charity run by people with OCD, for people with OCD. Includes facts, news and treatments.

Phone: 0333 212 7890 (Monday to Friday, 9am to 5pm)

Website: www.ocduk.org

PAPYRUS

Young suicide prevention society.

Phone: HOPElineUK 0800 068 4141 (Monday to Friday, 10am to 5pm and 7pm to 10pm, and 2pm to 5pm on weekends)

Website: www.papyrus-uk.org

Rethink Mental Illness

Support and advice for people living with mental illness.

Phone: 0300 5000 927 (Monday to Friday, 9.30am to 4pm)

Website: www.rethink.org

Samaritans

Confidential support for people experiencing feelings of distress or despair.

Phone: 116 123 (free 24-hour helpline)

Website: www.samaritans.org

SANE

Emotional support, information and guidance for people affected by mental illness, their families and carers.

SANEline: 0300 304 7000 (daily, 4.30pm to 10.30pm)

Textcare: comfort and care via text message, sent when the person needs it most: www.sane.org.uk/textcare

Peer support forum: www.sane.org.uk/supportforum

Website: www.sane.org.uk/support

YoungMinds

Information on child and adolescent mental health. Services for parents and professionals.

Phone: Parents' helpline 0808 802 5544 (Monday to Friday, 9.30am to 4pm)

Website: www.youngminds.org.uk

ABUSE (CHILD, SEXUAL, DOMESTIC VIOLENCE)

NSPCC

Children's charity dedicated to ending child abuse and child cruelty.

Phone: 0800 1111 for Childline for children (24-hour helpline)

0808 800 5000 for adults concerned about a child (24-hour helpline)

Website: www.nspcc.org.uk

Refuge

Advice on dealing with domestic violence.

Phone: 0808 2000 247 (24-hour helpline)

Website: www.refuge.org.uk

ADDICTION (DRUGS, ALCOHOL, GAMBLING)

Alcoholics Anonymous

Phone: 0800 917 7650 (24-hour helpline)

Website: www.alcoholics-anonymous.org.uk

Narcotics Anonymous

Phone: 0300 999 1212 (daily, 10am to midnight)

Website: www.ukna.org

National Gambling Helpline

Phone: 0808 8020 133 (daily, 8am to midnight)

Website: www.begambleaware.org

ALZHEIMER'S

Alzheimer's Society

Provides information on dementia, including factsheets and helplines.

Phone: 0300 222 1122 (Monday to Friday, 9am to 5pm, and 10am to 4pm on weekends)

Website: www.alzheimers.org.uk

BEREAVEMENT

Cruse Bereavement Care

Phone: 0808 808 1677 (Monday to Friday, 9am to 5pm)

Website: www.cruse.org.uk

CRIME VICTIMS

Rape Crisis

To find your local services phone:
0808 802 9999 (daily, 12pm to 2.30pm and 7pm to 9.30pm)

Website: www.rapecrisis.org.uk

Victim Support

Phone: 0808 168 9111 (24-hour helpline)

Website: www.victimsupport.org

EATING DISORDERS

Beat

Phone: 0808 801 0677 (for adults) or 0808 801 0711 (for under-18s)

Website: www.b-eat.co.uk

LEARNING DISABILITIES

Mencap

Charity working with people with a learning disability, their families and carers.

Phone: 0808 808 1111 (Monday to Friday, 9am to 5pm)

Website: www.mencap.org.uk

PARENTING

Family Lives

Advice on all aspects of parenting, including dealing with bullying.

Phone: 0808 800 2222 (Monday to Friday, 9am to 9pm and Saturday to Sunday, 10am to 3pm)

Website: www.familylives.org.uk

RELATIONSHIPS

Relate

The UK's largest provider of relationship support.

Website: www.relate.org.uk

ACKNOWLEDGEMENTS

I would like to thank everyone who has been part of *Ten Times Happier*. Special acknowledgement to my partner Mark for encouraging me to write a second book.

Likewise, to friends and family for their continuous support and belief in me. I am indebted to my amazing agent and friend, Bev James, who has been the most incredible source of inspiration, and of course to her lovely team. Sincere gratitude to Carver PR who are just simply the loveliest and best team I could hope to work with. Heartfelt thanks to everyone at HQ publishers, my new publishing family. Lisa Milton believed in the content and purpose of this book from our first meeting, and her enthusiasm filled me with excitement. Finally, I need to thank Rachel Kenny, my editor, for her amazing eye for details, and her patience. And for anyone I've missed, you know who you are. Thank you all for helping me get this book out in the world. I hope it will make a difference to the lives of many.